MY BUMPY RIDE
TO INNER PEACE

A CHINESE GRANDMOTHER'S TALE
OF FINDING CULTURAL BALANCE

Lian Henriksen

Copyright © 2024 by Lian Henriksen

All rights reserved. No part of this book may be used or reproduced by any means, graphic, electronic, or mechanical, including photocopying, recording, taping, or by any information storage retrieval system, without the written permission of the publisher except in the case of brief quotations embodied in critical articles and reviews.

Contents

Foreword 1

Chapter 1: Wrinkles 5

Chapter 2: Skinlessly Honest & Diplomacy 7

Chapter 3: My Beginnings & Beginnings in Denmark ... 10

Chapter 4: Brushes with Creation 15

Chapter 5: My Mother, Chew Chi Leng 19

Chapter 6: Motherhood 22

Chapter 7: My Two Sons and Pre-birth Planning & Soul Contracts 31

Chapter 8: My Life's Purpose: The Art of Softness 35

Chapter 9: The Men in My Life 38

Chapter 10: Healing of Self and DIY Healing 43

Chapter 11: My Siblings – The Conflicts & The Joys 48

Chapter 12: Popo, My Grandmother, Poverty, Humiliation & Psychic Connection 54

Chapter 13: My Father, His Father—Humiliation & Reconciliation 58

Chapter 14: My Life with My Father as I Recall 62

Chapter 15: My Relationship to Money 67

Chapter 16: My 78th Birthday – Gathering of The Clan at Porto, Portugal 71

Chapter 17: Aftermath of the Birthday Gathering: Regret, Reconciliation & Forgiveness 76

Chapter 18: Aging, Pain and Building A Legacy of Insight and Understanding 81

Chapter 19: My Ousting from Jenuine Healing and Forgiveness .. 85

Chapter 20: Cultural Conflicts in Names 90

Chapter 21: My Inner Child & The Power and Beauty of Self-Acceptance 93

Chapter 22: The Emotional Reflections on The Family Gathering Summer of July 2024 98

Chapter 23: My Soul Contracts with My Two Daughters 102

Chapter 24: Soul Contracts and Family Dynamics: Healing My Ancestral Lineage 105

Chapter 25: Inner Peace & Healing A War-Torn Legacy 109

Chapter 26: My Grandchildren & Seeding the Mycelium 116

Chapter 27: The Finished Family Tree & If I Must Die 122

Chapter 28: The Midwives of Peace 126

Afterword 128

Acknowledgments 130

Foreword

In the quiet moments of my mornings, a gentle urge to write began to grow, leading me on an unexpected journey. As a Chinese Grandmama living in the heart of Denmark, I sought wisdom and clarity on how best to share my experiences and thoughts. With guidance from the Council of Light and insights from the Akashic Records, I found the courage to embark on this path of storytelling.

In January 2021, when I first reached out for spiritual guidance, my intention was simple: to support others, especially women, in moving from a mindset of separation to unity. However, I also felt a deep need to address the complex and painful issues of racialism, slavery, and colonization. The advice I received was both encouraging and humbling, reminding me that these topics are now at the forefront of our collective consciousness. My words should come from a place of healing rather than intellect, focusing on mending the inner separation that echoes in our world.

This book is a humble offering of my story, shared in the hope that it might bring healing—not just to myself and my family, but to others who may read it. It is not a grand statement, but a simple, sincere reflection on the lessons I've learned. My wish is that through these pages, I can contribute to the healing and understanding our world so deeply needs and inspire you, the reader, to live with greater awareness and connection.

This is my story, shared with the hope that it may bring some insight, peace, or comfort to those who come across it.

Why You Should Listen to Me

You may wonder why my words are worth your time. Let me share the journey that has led me here and the experiences that qualify me to speak about **healing, transformation, and empowerment**.

I am not just a storyteller—I am someone who has walked the path of **personal and spiritual transformation**, and my journey has been shaped by years of both **study and practice**. My qualifications reflect a deep commitment to understanding the mind, body, and spirit, and to supporting others in their healing and personal growth.

Here are some of the key steps along my path:

- **SRT Mind & Energy Coach (2019)** – My training as an SRT (Subconscious Release Technique) coach enables me to help others clear energetic blocks and emotional patterns. I'm now fascinated with tools such as **Amy Jo Ellis's Full Court of Atonement, The Gene Keys, Map of Consciousness by Dr. David Hawkins,** and **The Sophia Code**.

- **Reiki and Schiem Master Teacher of the Dr. Mikao Usui Lineage (2018)** – As a Reiki Master Teacher, I have guided many in the practice of energy healing, helping them achieve **balance and wellness** through ancient techniques.

- **Law of Attraction Coach, QSCA (USA, 2013)** – This qualification allowed me to help others harness the power of their thoughts and intentions to manifest **positive changes** in their lives.

- **Awakening to Your Life's Potential & Living Your Supreme Destiny with Dr. Jean Houston (2011)** – My work with Dr. Houston opened my understanding of the **potential for** human transformation and helped me guide others in realizing their life's purpose.

- **Awakening & Mastery of Feminine Power with Claire Zammit & Katherine Woodward Thomas (2011)** – This training focused on the **empowerment of women**, helping them access their innate **strength and wisdom**.
- **Acupressurist (2003)** – Trained by the **Department of Traditional Medicine at Hanoi Medical College**, I learned to use acupressure for holistic healing, combining both traditional knowledge and modern techniques.
- **Ayurvedic Yoga Massage (2003)** – I was trained by **Sidhamo Michael Johnson** in Ayurvedic practices that help people restore balance through massage, breathwork, and stretching.
- **Hoffman Process – Inner Child Healing (1998)** – This process allowed me to go deep into **healing childhood wounds**, which greatly influenced my work in helping others transform emotional trauma.
- **Certified Healer by Charlotte Pedersen of the Bob Moore Lineage** – This training gave me a strong foundation in healing techniques passed down through generations, helping me facilitate healing for many.
- **Businesswoman – Owner/Director of Kiki Design AS (Closed in 2003)** – In addition to my healing work, I ran my own business for years, giving me a grounded understanding of the **challenges of leadership** and **entrepreneurship**.
- **ACIS Business Studies, London (1967)** – My formal business education laid the groundwork for my approach to

mentorship and coaching, helping me combine practical wisdom with spiritual insight.

Through these varied experiences, I have gained a **broad spectrum of tools and insights** that have helped me guide others toward **personal freedom** and **spiritual fulfillment**. I share this not to boast, but to assure you that my knowledge is based on **years of learning, practice, and transformation**—both my own and that of the many people I have worked with.

My journey has been about helping others step into their **power**, heal their **emotional wounds**, and **create the life they desire**. I hope the insights and stories in this book will help you on your own path to **wholeness** and **freedom**.

CHAPTER 1

Wrinkles

Written on 25th May 2023

Today is Josephine Gammeljord Henriksen's, my grandchild number two's birthday. She is 6. And I am embarking on the joyous journey of being a 'perfect' grandmother. As you would have noticed, I have put the word perfect in inverted commas, for I believe that the true joy lies in the imperfections of this journey.

I have use 365 Tao Daily Meditations since 26th January 2018, about six years ago. And today I re-read and re-contemplated Wrinkles #141 and it really inspired me to use it as my Introduction of my book.

"Wrinkles – the older one gets the more one is conscious of aging. When we look in the mirror, we reluctantly acknowledge the aging mask. It seems that there is no escaping the marks of life. Every experience that we have, everything that we do and think is registered upon us as surely as the steady embroidery of a tattoo artist. But to a large degree, the pattern and picture that will emerge is up to us.

In life, it is we who select what we will become by the actions we perform. There is no reason to go through life thoughtlessly and let accidents shape us. That is like allowing oneself to be tattooed by a blind man. How can you help but turn out old and ugly. Whether we emerge beautiful or ugly is our sole responsibility."

And today's meditation - #145 Views, has been so useful in this connection. It says: "There is a way to know Tao directly and completely. It requires the awakening of one's spiritual force. When this happens, spirituality manifests as a bright light. Your mind expands as a glowing presence. Like a lighthouse, this beacon of energy becomes illumination and the eye at the same time. Significantly, however, what it shows, it also knows directly. It is the light that sees."

What an incredible goal, what a fantastic destiny, what an amazing higher purpose!

CHAPTER 2

Skinlessly Honest & Diplomacy

Written on 25th May 2023 and 12th October 2024

In Danish, there's a term—*hudløse ærlig*—which translates directly to "skinlessly honest." This phrase is about being so true to oneself that there is no mask, no pretense. When I asked my English brother-in-law, Kenneth, for an equivalent term in English, we found ourselves in an unexpected reflection on honesty and authenticity.

Kenneth reminded me that **English culture often masks honesty with politeness**. "Being authentic in English is seen as socially maladroit," he wrote, which means it can seem clumsy, even impolite, to be fully transparent. To this, I replied that my life's purpose is to be kind, honest, and true to myself—yet I could see how this had sometimes led to conflict. Authenticity, I reflected, does not always lead to peace.

Over the years, I have faced the question: **Is being authentically myself worth the risks?** My commitment to honesty has sometimes estranged me from my family. In 2024, I wonder if being fully real is worth putting myself in a position to be hurt or criticized. **Can I live "skinlessly" and still find acceptance and peace?**

The Role of Gene Key #6: Conflict and Diplomacy

This morning 12th October 2024, I felt an impulse to contemplate **Gene Key #6** again. This Gene Key speaks to the transformation from the **shadow of Conflict** to the **Gift of Diplomacy** and, ultimately, to the **Siddhi of Peace**. It made me reflect on my journey through honesty, conflict, and the search for peace in a new light.

Diplomacy, as **Gene Key #6** teaches, is the art of knowing when to speak, when to listen, when to act, and when to pause. It is about sensing the energy of a situation and choosing a course of action that aligns with higher harmony, rather than simply reacting out of impulse. This insight was a revelation for me. It showed me that **honesty does not have to be at odds with peace**—if approached with the **grace of diplomacy**.

For so long, I had associated **being authentic** with speaking my truth openly, regardless of the consequences. But this contemplation of **Gene Key #6** reminded me that **authenticity and diplomacy** can coexist. I realized that while being "skinlessly honest" means removing the mask, it does not mean abandoning wisdom in how we communicate that truth.

Balancing Authenticity and Peace

What a gift to be reminded of this delicate balance. **Diplomacy** does not mean hiding behind masks or avoiding difficult truths; rather, it is the art of **navigating conflict with grace**, knowing that truth can be expressed in a way that fosters understanding and connection, rather than division.

As I reflect on the path from **Conflict to Peace**, I now see that the question is not simply whether I can be authentically myself—it's about **how** I express that authenticity. By embracing the principles of **Gene Key #6**, I can be true to myself and still cultivate peace, both within myself and in my relationships.

This realization has shifted my perspective. **Authenticity**, I now understand, does not mean throwing away the possibility of connection or peace. Instead, it is about expressing who we truly are while remaining open to the **flow of diplomacy** and the wisdom that comes from **listening deeply** to ourselves and others.

CHAPTER 3

My Beginnings & Beginnings in Denmark

Written on 15th March 2021

In Malaysia, where I originate from, there are three major racial groups: Malays (53%), Chinese (35%), and Indians (10.6%). There is a common stereotype that Malays were predominantly farmers, Chinese were traders, and Indians worked as rubber estate laborers. Unfortunately, many Chinese, including myself, have felt a sense of superiority and have historically believed that economic success is tied to a strong command of the English language and a reverence for the white man. This mindset was deeply ingrained in me and took years to change.

I was born in Singapore on 8 July 1945, just 30 days before World War II was declared over. My entry into the world was dramatic—my mother was suffering from malaria, and my grandmother, a fisherwoman, found ice to keep her temperature down. This early experience of survival set the tone for my life. The midwife held my legs and clapped my bottom for an hour before I made my first sound. My mother told me this story, and I have never forgotten it.

As the eldest of four daughters, I grew up in a cultural context where having only girls was not seen as a blessing. My mother told me that my father's estate workers even offered their sons for adoption.

My father, Cyril, was a rubber planter living on an estate near Bakri, a village 12 miles from Muar. Bakri was considered dangerous due to the presence of Chinese communists. When we visited my father, we traveled in an armored car to protect us from ambushes. Our home in Bakri was guarded by soldiers 24/7, even after the government declared the 'Emergency' over in July 1960. Shortly afterward, we moved to Bakri Estate but continued our schooling in Muar.

My father, who didn't even have a Chinese name, introduced us to Western culture early on, exposing us to classical music and Western philosophy. He sent all four of us to universities abroad, not just to give us better career opportunities, but also to help us find better husbands. My father has always believed that a woman's place is in the home. And that it is a man's job to provide for his family.

In 1969, I married a Chinese man and had two children before divorcing in 1978. A year later, I married a Dane I met in Singapore. This second marriage took me to China in 1979, where my husband, Bjørn, was asked to head the Chinese department of the Danish East Asiatic Company. To facilitate this move, I gave up my Malaysian citizenship for a Danish passport, as neither country allowed dual citizenship at the time. Looking back, it was a bold move, but perhaps one of the most foolish decisions I ever made.

Living in China was a profound experience. We stayed at the Peking Hotel because foreigners were not allowed to rent houses. Our chauffeur turned out to be a spy. The uniformity of life there struck me deeply—millions of bicycles, people dressed in identical Mao uniforms and shoes, and the constant surveillance by crowds standing in front of the hotel. It was uncomfortable and disheartening. Bjørn once offered to buy me a white mink coat, but I refused. It felt wrong to wear mink in Peking, China, not because of the minks, but because it seemed so out of place.

There are many memories from my time in China: cooking in a micro-oven we pretended was a small TV, the monotony of the food, the grey skies of Peking, and the sadness etched on people's faces. This sadness lingers in me even now as I write.

My son Kim, who was 18 months old at the time, was with us in Peking. We spent our days walking around the city and in the nearby gardens. One vivid memory is when Kim fell into a freezing pond. I fished him out, and Bjørn, who appeared seemingly out of nowhere, quickly covered him with his jacket. Kim doesn't remember this, but I feel that experience is somehow embedded in his DNA.

On weekends, we would have picnics in the gardens. The one I remember best was the grounds of an old summer palace, once belonging to Chinese royalty, now reduced to peach and plum blossom trees after being plundered and burned by the British. It was here that my interest in Chinese history began. I read about the Opium Wars and learned how the Chinese were humiliated by the British Empire.

During one of our walks, a young Chinese boy approached me to buy antiques. I was intrigued and embarked on a dramatic journey, changing taxis several times before buying about 60 snuff bottles. I kept half and gave the other half to Kim's father. I still have a vase made of oxblood glaze.

The memories of China stirred a deep sense of resentment in me, which lingers even now. Reflecting on these experiences, I recall how deeply I was affected by the living conditions of the people—the drab quarters, the coal-heated rooms, the hard mud floors. It was all very sad and somewhat traumatic. After two years, Bjørn decided it was time to return to Copenhagen. We moved back to Denmark in 1980 when I was 35.

The experiences I gathered in China stayed in the background until the Dalai Lama visited Denmark in 2009. The Danish government did not officially meet with him to avoid offending China, a key trading partner. I was also concerned about China's influence, particularly their purchase of shares in large Danish companies. Though I never verified these concerns, the question lingered in my mind—would the Chinese people ever seek revenge for the humiliation they suffered under the white man?

Then, in January 2020, COVID-19 broke out. It was said to have originated in Wuhan from a bat. Jane Goodall's theories made me wonder about the Chinese insensitivity to wild animals, something I found disgusting. I remember a TV show about Chinese people putting live cats into boiling water before skinning them. My son, Kim, remarked, "This is the only time I am ashamed of my Chinese ancestry."

The US elections followed, throwing me off balance. As a partner in SRT Global, a company promoting peace, I became increasingly aware of the concept of the Cabal—a small group of elites allegedly controlling the world. The COVID-19 lockdown only added to my confusion, and nothing seemed to make sense.

In December 2020, I had the privilege of connecting with Jeshua through Pamela Kribbe in a webinar organized by Droga Mistrzostwa (Way of Mastery). I thanked Jeshua for sharing his experience of shock when he entered the physical Earth over 2,000 years ago. This resonated with me deeply. In connection with COVID-19, I asked him about the purpose of the separation that has been exacerbated by the pandemic. Jeshua's response was insightful:

"Governments worldwide are battling this virus with regulations and restrictions, sparking much discussion. I ask you to disconnect from political debates, as they can endlessly distract you. There is no easy answer. From a spiritual perspective, consider this: What do my social connections actually mean to me? Distinguish between the lack of social connections and the lack of connection with yourself—your true self, your soul. From a broader perspective, this is what Earth and humanity need right now. People must go deep within to address the original pain that drives them to constantly search and distract themselves. Many global problems stem from this disconnection from the soul. This crisis is happening for a reason, and the most productive way to view it is to focus on yourself and ask: 'What is this time inviting me to do or challenging me to do?'"

This reflection led me to focus on financial freedom, as I believe it is essential for pursuing both personal and spiritual freedom.

CHAPTER 4

Brushes with Creation

Written on 2021.06.22

In the quiet of my morning stillness, I often converse with Creation, seeking guidance and clarity. Lately, this question has been burning within me:

Dear Creation,

Is my destiny to be a teacher, guiding people to become best friends with their souls? Should I spend the rest of my time on earth being a living example that the Material and the Spirit can be integrated, and to do that, do I need to fully understand the Universal Laws?

Your Humble Servant,

Gladys Lian

This morning, as I revisited the introduction to the Aquarian Age, I felt compelled to reflect on my first brush with Creation.

My First Brush with Creation

On April 19, 1979, my third child, Kim, was born via cesarean section at Singapore Gleneagles Hospital. It was during this moment that I first encountered Creation—not the Creator, but the vast, enigmatic force that shapes our existence. I vividly remember hurtling through a bright tunnel, acutely aware of the danger to Kim's life. In that moment, I bargained with Creation: "You can't take him away. His father hasn't even seen him." I promised to baptize Kim if he was allowed to live. Soon after, I learned that Kim's lungs had failed to open, and he was urgently transferred to Singapore General Hospital. For the first ten days of his life, he remained in an incubator, while I stayed at Gleneagles. It was later revealed that Kim had been delivered 30 days prematurely due to a miscalculation of his due date. In hindsight, I realized the importance of trusting the natural process. Kim was eventually baptized at Bagsværd Church and, despite occasional asthma, he thrives today.

A Second Encounter

My second brush with Creation occurred in 1988, shortly after Bjørn left me. I attended a healing workshop with Charlotte Pedersen while still living in Bagsværd. During the workshop, we were asked to create clay figures of ourselves while blindfolded. When I removed my blindfold, I was surprised to see that my clay figure was standing upright, glowing with a deep yellow light. This light stayed with me for a long time, a reminder of something beyond my understanding. That evening, I experienced something that frightened me—a haunting by The Eye. These eyes, some larger than others, appeared everywhere for about 30 minutes. The next day, Charlotte reassured me not to be afraid. Since then, I have occasionally seen this light in my meditations and reiki massages, but the eyes have never returned, though I wish they would.

A Third Encounter

In August 1999, after undergoing surgery for cancer, I traveled to London to participate in the Hoffman Process, a workshop designed to address and transform the negative effects of childhood experiences. During this trip, I encountered something that felt like a message from God. While walking, I came across a solitary "monolith." With my father's book, *In Search of Stones* by M. Scott Peck, MD, in hand, I couldn't help but think this encounter was significant. As I approached the monolith, I discovered a small, narrow hole and used a twig to explore it. To my surprise, I found a medallion with the figure of St. George. I kept it but later replaced it with a Danish 20-kroner coin, as advised by my sister in Singapore. Unfortunately, the medallion was stolen in 2003 while I was traveling from Hanoi to Bat Trang, a pottery village. Yet, the memory of that encounter remains with me.

A Fourth Encounter

In September 2016, during an Ayahuasca/Natem medicine ceremony, I had a profound experience with Creation. After releasing a primal scream, I was shown a psychedelic image of the Universe—a beautiful, infinite geodesic dome, filled with magical colors. This vision of interconnectedness resonated deeply with me, affirming the unity of all things.

Journeys of Discovery

Inspired by this revelation, I embarked on three significant journeys in 2018:

1. **Jerusalem/Bethlehem/Tel Aviv**: Arriving in Bethlehem on December 23, 2017, and leaving Tel Aviv on January 3, 2018, I sought to understand the Palestine Conflict. The discomfort I felt in Bethlehem contrasted with the ease I found in Tel Aviv, leaving me puzzled.

2. **Egypt (Aswan-Luxor-Cairo)**: From April 11 to 24, 2018, I traveled with Pamela Kribbe, who channels Jeshua, to explore ancient mysteries and spiritual truths.

3. **Iceland (Reykjavik, The Journey of The Womb)**: From July 23 to 30, 2018, I delved into the feminine mysteries and the sacredness of the womb.

Through these journeys, I began to understand that any conflict, such as the one in Palestine, is a reflection of the conflicts within myself. I realized that my feelings are often shaped by external influences—media, social narratives, and biased information. My spirit guides advised me to seek truth through my own diligence, rather than relying on external sources.

A Path of Neutrality

Since these encounters, I have focused on maintaining a vibration of neutrality, striving to be aware of my moment-to-moment prejudices. I have come to see that remaining neutral allows for a clearer connection with Creation, unclouded by the biases of the material world.

Looking Ahead

As I continue on this path of inner growth, I eagerly anticipate more brushes with Creation. Each encounter has brought me closer to understanding the delicate balance between the Material and the Spirit, and I remain committed to exploring this integration in my life.

CHAPTER 5

My Mother, Chew Chi Leng

Written on 6th March 2023

"I am a strong woman because a strong woman raised me. Thank you, Mother—the sassiest woman I know."

My mother passed away as a multi-millionaire. Not bad for a woman who was born without a name and walked 10 kilometers to school, wearing shoes with holes. The life I lead today is a testament to the qualities I inherited from her, as well as the financial support she left behind.

Born in Singapore on May 15, 1925, my mother's childhood was far from easy. Her own mother, my Popo, was a fisherwoman who owned fish traps called kelongs and had little time for her. Raised by a caregiver who treated her poorly, my mother nonetheless excelled in her studies at Fairfield Girls' School. Her education, however, was abruptly interrupted in February 1942 when the war began, and Singapore was occupied. Although she seldom spoke about this period, I knew she became fluent in Japanese.

In late 1944, she met my father, and they married soon after. I was born not long after, on July 8, 1945, at 5:10 PM in Singapore's Kadang Kerbau Hospital. My mother nearly lost her life during my birth due to malaria. My grandmother, Popo, who through her connections as a fisherwoman , managed to gather ice to keep my mother's temperature down. My father was away on the island of Palau Betam for work, so it was Uncle Charlie who accompanied her to the hospital.

My mother rarely spoke about the war, but she did share that her father was deeply affected by the bombing of Singapore, to the point of madness. She recounted how he would boil rice to feed lost souls.

After the war, my mother wanted to resume her studies, but the principal of Fairfield Girls' School refused her re-admittance, citing her new role as a mother. Instead, she became the wife of a rubber planter, my father, Cyril Chew. Life was difficult, as she had to care not only for me but also for my father's younger sisters, Phyllis and Nancy, who had lost their mother during the war.

Throughout her life, my mother followed my father wherever his career took him—Batu Pahat, Muar, Bakri, Scudai, and finally Johore Bahru. She played an active role in managing my father's small rubber holdings. The memories of my mother driving around in a Land Rover, collecting latex from Hope Estate, and transporting it to the latex collection tank remain vivid in my mind.

I also clearly remember how my mother participated in planter's parties, social events at Tanjong Club Muar, and even entered and won a beauty contest, earning the title of Miss Muar.

Despite her vibrant public life, my mother lived under my father's dominating nature for as long as I can remember. Two incidents stand out vividly in my memory, both occurring at Jalan Waspada, Johore Bahru. The first was just after a disagreement with my father. She told me, "I never left your father because of you four children." I responded, "We left home ages ago. Lillian, your youngest daughter, left 20 years ago." The second conversation took place shortly after my father died in February 2007. She confided in me, "I don't miss your father." I advised her, "Even if it's true, I wouldn't go around saying it to other people." Yet, despite these sentiments, she insisted on keeping half of my father's ashes in an urn and eventually buried them in the garden.

Through our many conversations, it became clear that one of her deepest regrets was not fulfilling her dream of becoming a medical doctor. I believe she secretly wished that one of her daughters would pursue that path. I still vividly recall the irritation I felt whenever she mentioned that someone's daughter had just become a doctor.

In 2011, at my sister's request, my mother moved to Singapore. A few short years later, on May 12, 2015, she chose to leave this world at the age of 90. Watching her grow both mentally and physically weak in the last six months of her life was one of the most difficult experiences for me.

She was buried at sea, with my father's ashes buried alongside her—a final gesture that revealed the depth of her love for him, a gesture that will stay with me forever.

During a Chew family reunion in Bali in 2001, when everyone present was asked to read a poem or share something meaningful, this is what my mother chose:

LET US DO IT NOW!

I shall pass through this world but once. Any good thing therefore I can do or any kindness I can show to any human being, let me do it now. Let me not defer or neglect it. For I shall never pass this way again.

Even now, I often wonder what her next incarnation will be. My mother, the sassiest woman I have ever known!

CHAPTER 6

Motherhood

Written on 1st April 2021
Reflections on Motherhood

What does it mean to be a good mother? This question has challenged me deeply, particularly in my relationships with my two sons, Kenneth, my firstborn, and Kim, my second son and third born.

During my silent hour today, I meditated on fear, inspired by meditation number 78 from *365 Tao Daily Meditations*, one of my guiding 'bibles':

"Trust the gods within,
Accept given boons
Illusion is reality's border:
Pierce fear to go beyond"

In your meditations, you will meet gods. These gods are nothing more than the holiest aspects of your own mind; they are not other beings. Your inner gods will grant gifts of knowledge and power. Accept what comes your way without doubt, without fear, for you can trust your gods. They will never destroy you, for you cannot destroy yourself.

Such trust dissolves fear and regret. You will find a resolution to your inner conflicts. The gods will direct you forward to the very border of reality itself. On the other side is vast profundity and the ultimate nature of existence. But the border can only be crossed if you have resolved all fear and regret."

Resolving fear has been a journey I've been on for the past 18 years, but resolving regret is something new. One of my deepest regrets is that I abandoned my son Kenneth when he was 7 and my daughter Jo-Ann when she was 5. This regret lingers in my heart, alongside another—giving up my Malaysian citizenship. The question that haunts me is whether I am forgivable for these decisions.

Challenges with My Two Sons

On Kenneth's 50th birthday, March 11, 2021, I wrote him a letter:

Dear Kenneth,

Tomorrow is your 50th birthday. I've tried this before, and I'm trying again today. What will it take for you to forgive your mother for whatever sins I have committed against you? Would giving you a sum of money help? Would that allow you to release your anger and grudges? Do you need to hear the full story behind your father's and my divorce? Would you like to hear my side of the story?

The last time, just before Linda's birthday in Bali, I wanted to spend some time with you and Blade, but you refused. You wouldn't even make eye contact with me in Bali.

So, my son, what act of atonement would you like from me? Please let me know. Bearing so much sadness and anger is not good for you, especially for your health.

I hope you have a good birthday celebration with Blade and Julie, with lots of good food. I hope to hear from you soon.

Love,

Your Mother

Kenneth's reply that same day was a mix of gratitude and unresolved emotions:

Dear Mom,

Thank you for your birthday wishes and for sending a thoughtful email reaching out to me. In my younger days, I never thought I'd make it to this milestone.

We'll go out for a simple dinner tonight—a treat these days, as we've had to endure a lifestyle change due to a significant pay cut from COVID-19's impact on the economy.

I'll reflect on this more closely, as the reason for my anger and unhappiness isn't clear to me anymore. I'm almost certain it's not about you leaving us when I was 7. I also know you and Kong Kong tried several times to get Jo and me out of our horrible situation. My anger from that period is directed squarely at Catherine. I'll let you know when I understand my own feelings a little better.

I'll also let you know if I'd like to take you up on any of your offers.

Love,

Ken

I responded, expressing my gratitude and lingering regret:

Dearest Ken,

Thank you so much for your response. I'm grateful to know that you're thinking about how to forgive me. My only regret in life is that I didn't secure complete custody of you and Jo, while your father got the house. Why else would Popo and Kong Kong have agreed to look after you both until I was more settled? It broke your grandfather's heart that his hands were tied when I lost everything by giving up my Malaysian citizenship.

I'd like to send you some money as a birthday gift—perhaps you can buy something you need. Please let me know how—PayPal or your bank account number.

I'm sorry to hear about the pay cut.

Love,

Your Mother

Kenneth never gave me a reply. Neither did I follow up.

An incident occurred on Christmas December 25, 2020 with my son no.2 Kim. After the Christmas dinner, I was told that it was stupid and out of place to give his in-laws crystals as Christmas presents. This led me to send an SMS to Kim that I have since regretted.

I am sick and tired of you. Goodbye.

In hindsight, I wish I had said something more reflective:

"I'm sorry, my son. But I'm old enough to be who I am and not have you tell me what I can or cannot do with your in-laws."

After almost three months of silence, I reached out to Kim on March 13, 2021:

Dear Kim, Karen just told me about your change in number. I trust all is well with your new job. I wanted to let you know that I have the Kaj Bøjsen cutlery you wanted. It's a present for both you and Victoria—an early birthday gift for you and one for Victoria later this month. Do you want to pick it up one of these days?

Kim's response on March 17, 2021, was a request for a deeper conversation:

Dear Mom,

Thank you for reaching out and for buying us a nice gift. Of course, we can arrange a handover, but I think it would be more suitable to have a talk. I'm very sad about how our relationship has developed over the years and how I feel you are more interested in preaching your spiritual views than being a mother. Are you willing to have this conversation with me with an open mind?

I replied the next day, with a mix of frustration and resignation:

Well, Kim—an open mind? What is your definition of that? A good mother? What is your definition of that? Kim, I can accept that you think I'm wacko. More, I don't have to say. I'm very happy that you're doing well with Victoria, your daughter, your job, your father, and your in-laws. That I'm more interested in preaching my spiritual views than being a mother... hmmm!

Kim's response was direct:

How can you be offended by this? You've always declared how important your work/journey/beliefs are to you. You're not interested in talking about things that don't interest you. You always try to convince us of your spiritual views. You also refused to get a COVID test for Christmas because you don't believe in it, even knowing your son has a chronic lung disease. But if you don't want to talk, that's your choice. But please stop the narrative that I don't need you anymore now that I'm happy with my family, job, and in-laws. That's simply not true.

On March 19, 2021, I sent a final SMS to Kim:

All I want to say is: I'm sorry—please forgive me—thank you—I love you for not being the mother you think you needed. Remember, Kim, you are almost 42. I'm sorry I didn't want to be tested for COVID-19 before your Christmas party, and I'm sorry that I'm not getting vaccinated now. I'm sorry. I'm sorry your old mother really tried her best to be a good mother to you and Karen. I'll send the cutlery through Karen so she can give it to you.

Kim's response was brief:

You're not even trying.

I replied:

Trying what? To be a good mother from your perspective? What do you want me to do? You're welcome to come to my home to talk if that would help. Would you? I honestly want to know.

As of March 31, 2021, I haven't heard from Kim.

Spiritual Insights on Motherhood

As I reflect on these exchanges, I'm reminded of the channeling of Mother Mary by Pamela Kribbe on spiritual motherhood. Mother Mary spoke of how, even in her struggles, she knew her presence influenced all life around her. She realized that her true mission was to focus on herself and the integrity of her being, allowing light to flow through her to others.

Mother Mary's greatest achievement, she said, was releasing Jeshua and letting him be who he was. Her most challenging task was learning to be a spiritual mother and letting go of the emotions tied to earthly motherhood.

How Do I Relate This to My Sons?

What does it mean to be a spiritual mother to myself? What do I need to let go of in my role as a mother? As I ask these questions, I also reflect on my own mother's way of mothering—her anxiety, her overbearing nature, and her controlling tendencies. How much of my resentment toward her do I need to release?

Mother Mary's message from *The Sophia Code* resonates deeply with me:

"You are struggling intensely with certain negative parts of yourself. These are emotional blockages or negative beliefs about yourself. Try to look at them with the eye of a spiritual mother: not a mother who wants to solve everything, but a mother who sees you, who recognizes your unique energy. A mother who doesn't want to change you but honors you for who you are. You are meant to be spiritual mothers to the Christ child within."

"You can access the energy of spiritual motherhood by stopping trying to solve your problems for a moment and just looking at them, letting them be for a while. Can you muster a sense of love and appreciation for yourself while you are having this problem? That is a start."

"Do you remember how you looked at your newborn sons? Do you dare to look at yourself this way?"

Mother Mary continues:

"Realize now how you have been walking your own path, all your life, and how you have always tried to build a satisfactory reality for yourself. Even when you make mistakes, as you call them, you are trying your very best to create happiness or to find a way out of pain and despair. Give yourself a break for a while and generously allow yourself these mistakes. You are not here to be perfect. You are here to live, to experience, and to move through your experiences with a sense of wonder, even if they are negative. The worst thing that can happen to you as a human being is when you are not moving

anymore and when you are not open to new experiences. This happens when you feel completely stuck inside a problem or a belief system. When you feel completely stuck, then you are spiritually dead. There is no space anymore, no air to breathe, no sense of wonder in your life."

This morning, on April 1, 2021, less than 10 hours after finishing a clearing, I received a video and two photos of my granddaughter Augusta. I was deeply touched and, after thanking my daughter-in-law Victoria, I received an SMS that said, "Augusta looks like him."

Such synchronicity? I think not.

I have always loved this poem and still do:

On Children
Kahlil Gibran
1883 – 1931
And a woman who held a babe against her bosom said, Speak to us of Children.
And he said:
Your children are not your children.
They are the sons and daughters of Life's longing for itself.
They come through you but not from you,
And though they are with you yet they belong not to you.
You may give them your love but not your thoughts,
For they have their own thoughts.
You may house their bodies but not their souls,
For their souls dwell in the house of tomorrow, which you cannot visit, not even in your dreams.
You may strive to be like them, but seek not to make them like you.
For life goes not backward nor tarries with yesterday.

You are the bows from which your children as living arrows are sent forth.
The archer sees the mark upon the path of the infinite, and He bends you with His might that His arrows may go swift and far.
Let your bending in the archer's hand be for gladness;
For even as He loves the arrow that flies, so He loves also the bow that is stable.

CHAPTER 7

My Two Sons and Pre-birth Planning & Soul Contracts

Written on 1st March 2023

This morning, during my silent hour, I felt an impulse to reflect on soul contracts, reincarnation, and pre-birth planning, especially in connection with my children.

My Beliefs About the Soul and Life

These are the basic beliefs that guide my understanding:

1. **I am originally a spirit.** I chose to be embodied in a material body briefly to testify to the nature of the soul, who I am as a spirit, and the nature of Creation.

2. **There never was and never will be a single truth,** because it denies the right to choose.

3. **Life is like a game,** much like Monopoly. Each person starts at the beginning—birth—carrying a roadmap that outlines their destiny. This roadmap includes both predetermined paths and choices made along the way. As we play this game, we experience changes, make decisions, build relationships, and navigate ups and downs. Eventually, the game ends—symbolizing death and the return of the soul to its origin, Creation. Then, the cycle begins anew, with the soul being reborn in a new body or remaining as a spirit, starting a fresh journey elsewhere in the infinite universe.

4. **In my original source, I was not a soul,** but a small ball of light. A soul resides within a living being; a spirit is when the soul is outside the body.

5. **We choose our parents.** This is something I've always intuitively known. However, it wasn't until 2014, when I was guided to read *Your Soul's Gift* by Robert Schwartz, that I became aware of pre-birth planning and soul contracts. Accepting this concept helped me see how the events of my life have woven together for a purpose.

My Sons and the Challenges of Motherhood

Raising all four of my children has been quite a challenge, but today, I want to focus on my adult sons. My eldest son, Kenneth, is 53 years old, and his father is Malaysian Chinese. My second son, Kim, is 43 years old, and his father is Danish. Both of them find it amusing that I believe they chose me to be their mother, and that I agreed to be their mother for a reason.

Soul Contracts and Past Lives

In 2017, while I was on my way to Bali, I asked Kenneth if I could visit him in Kuala Lumpur and spend time with him and my grandson, Blade. He said no. Then, at my sister's 70th birthday party in Bali, Kenneth blatantly ignored me and refused to make eye contact. Later, on December 25, 2020, Kim not only criticized my behavior but also belittled the gift of crystals I gave at the Christmas party where I met his in-laws for the first time. These experiences left me deeply unsettled for a long time. In seeking guidance, I turned to a clairvoyant named Nadia. Her reading on January 19, 2021, marked a crucial turning point in my journey.

Kenneth and Guilt & Shame

During the reading, I learned that my soul and Kenneth's soul were connected in a past life approximately 4,500 years ago. In that lifetime, I lived in what is now Mongolia. I experienced the devastating loss of a child who had wandered away and never returned. This loss consumed me, leading me to spend the rest of my life searching for that child, to the detriment of my other children. I was haunted by the question of what I could have done differently to prevent the child from wandering away.

Nadia asked my soul why I needed to experience the trauma of losing a child. She then connected to an incarnation 7,000 years ago, where I lived near what is now Northern Russia. I belonged to a small and fierce tribe. Due to a shortage of food, we migrated south and encountered another group. In that lifetime, I was a murderer who deprived mothers of their children—an act that had left a heavy karmic imprint on my soul.

Nadia noted that Kenneth carried a strong and heavy karmic energy, but she couldn't fully discern the reason behind it. She needed Kenneth's consent to access and examine his soul contract for more insight. I am slowly beginning to understand the significance of soul contracts.

Kenneth is here to help me work through and heal my guilt, and to learn to love myself. He's also here to help me understand that I didn't abandon him when I left his father, and that it was okay to choose to leave a man whose core values didn't align with mine.

Kim and My Lessons in The Importance of Standing in My Essence

Nadia told me that my son's role in my life is to be a catalyst for my inner strength. The more I embrace my true self, the more he will be able to do the same. But Kim, he's a different kind of teacher. He's here to show me the power of self-belief, the freedom of living without a facade, and the beauty of truth and authenticity. He's here to guide me to that deep, unshakeable sense of self that remains when all external roles, expectations, and influences are stripped away-the part of me that feels most authentic and aligned with my inner truth.

After the clairvoyant reading, it became clear that I should anticipate numerous challenges and setbacks when my book is published. However, I am determined to stand firm in the knowledge that the contents of the book come from a place of healing rather than seeking attention for myself. Additionally, it was emphasized that being "skinlessly honest" is crucial, and I am committed to embodying authenticity and transparency in my creative endeavors.

The reading also reinforced the interconnected nature of self-deception, self-betrayal, and self-hate, highlighting the crucial need to embrace our true selves for healing.

CHAPTER 8

My Life's Purpose: The Art of Softness

Written on 1st March 2023

I once believed my life's purpose was to be a wife and mother with a traditional happy family. But after two divorces, I began to doubt this was the path for me. In 2011, I took courses with Dr. Jean Houston on Awakening to Your Life Purpose and Living Your Destiny, but nothing truly resonated.

In 2018, a Human Design specialist, Karen McMullun, told me that I was a Manifestor—one of the rarest types, making up only 9% of the population. Manifestors are designed to initiate and bring ideas to life, with a strong, independent energy. I was reminded of my innate leadership power, my tendency to act quickly and decisively, and the need for clear communication to inform others of my actions.

But being a Manifestor comes with its challenges. I learned that we carry a dense and repelling aura that can make us seem "too much" for others, causing them to react with discomfort or even resistance. This energy, though powerful for initiating, can also make Manifestors seem unreachable or overwhelming. It explains why, at times, I've felt like my presence alone was enough to alienate those around me. This "repelling" quality, which can push people away, often led me to question whether my energy was too forceful or incompatible with my relationships.

While Human Design gave me some insight into my energy dynamics, I still felt something was missing. Was this dense aura truly my path? Was my life's purpose really about initiating and leading, despite how isolating that often felt?

Softness Through Gene Key 57

In 2022, I was introduced to Gene Keys, and upon having my profile done, I discovered that Gene Key 57, known as The Gentle Wind, guides my life's purpose. According to Gene Key 57, my role is to bring the spirit of surrender and softness to the world, showing the power of yielding, listening deeply, and waiting with patience. This resonated deeply with me. It felt like a much-needed reminder in a world that constantly encourages us to push forward with force and determination.

For so long, I had believed that force was necessary—that being a Manifestor meant moving the world by initiating, even if that sometimes left me feeling alienated. But Gene Key 57 opened up a new possibility: that softness, not force, could be my true strength. In a world that often reacts to my dense aura with resistance, yielding could become my path to harmony. It was a shift from the external initiation of the Manifestor to the internal wisdom of softness and surrender.

From "Too Much" to Surrender

This realization made me reflect on how often I've been told I was "too much"—whether by family, colleagues, or even in personal relationships. My Manifestor energy may have felt overpowering, but this new understanding of my Gene Key showed me that the key to my purpose isn't about pushing harder; it's about letting go. Softness is not about being weak; it is about listening to the subtle winds of life, waiting for the right moment, and allowing others to come toward me, rather than being pushed away by the force of my presence.

Is this what Teri Uktena, an Akashic Record specialist, meant during a reading in 2021 when she described me as a very old soul? She said I was seeding updated codes into the world, much like upgrading a computer system. Her insight made me realize that my purpose may be to contribute to the evolution of the world—but not by initiating with force. Instead, I am here to embody softness, patience, and surrender.

Seeding the Future with Softness

This purpose of "seeding updated behavioral codes" in a spirit of surrender and softness resonates deeply with who I am today. It aligns with the understanding that, even as a Manifestor, my true power comes not from my ability to push forward, but from my ability to listen, yield, and guide others toward harmony through gentleness.

What once felt like a burden—my dense, repelling aura—has now become something I can soften. In this softness, I find a new purpose: to seed the future not by force, but by embodying the quiet strength of the Gentle Wind.

CHAPTER 9

The Men in My Life

Written on 1st January 2021

The foundation of my relationships with men was laid by my father, and I must admit, it's a complex story. My father's quest for the true purpose of life sparked my curiosity, yet he was also a commanding figure with a traditional view of women. I believe my subconscious yearning for his validation became a recurring theme in my relationships with men. The only time I truly earned his acknowledgment was when my second husband left me for another woman, and I held onto my dignity. I can still vividly recall his words: "I now understand why you always aspired to be an independent successful businesswoman."

In April 1999, I underwent surgery for cancer of the womb. As I refused mainstream after-care treatment, I looked into alternatives. Although I believed a passionate love affair was the cause of my illness, it was the recurring dreams about my childhood during my recovery that led me to explore the mind-body-spirit connection more deeply.

A brochure from my sister Linda introduced me to the Hoffman Quadrinity Process, and in August 1999, I attended an intensive course in London. This began a kind of "love affair" with both my father and mother that continued until New Year's Eve 2016/17. By that time, I had found forgiveness—for them and for myself.

But my journey with men didn't end there.

For years, I had worked on understanding why my relationships with men (and even money) always seemed to turn sour. I kept asking myself: *What is it about me that attracts these destructive patterns?*

I explored many angles:

- Am I too masculine or not feminine enough?
- Am I trapped in a patriarchal culture?
- Do I give too much or too little?
- Am I too emotional, or am I too cold?

None of these questions seemed to offer a clear answer. Then, partner No. 4 came along. His sudden abandonment in December 2008 left me financially crippled once again. For four and a half years, I avoided relationships altogether.

But in May 2013, I came across a passage in Barry Long's book *Making Love: Sexual Love the Divine Way* that deeply resonated with me. It spoke of the disconnect between men and women in modern society—how men had forgotten how to make love, and how this forgetfulness had led to both physical and emotional imbalances in women. I was curious, and so I re-entered the dating scene, hoping to discover if there was truth to this. The journey that followed was a roller coaster.

One breakthrough came about a year ago. I was in a long-term relationship with a man who had left and returned three times. One morning, during a moment of reflection, he sent me an SMS saying he could no longer trust me because I wasn't "woman enough." He mentioned that he needed to bring other women into our relationship.

That was the moment the camel's back broke. I told him to leave in no uncertain terms, and I haven't seen him since.

What surprised me was how good I felt afterward. For the first time, I felt completely free—free from needing validation from men and free from the belief that I needed a man to feel complete. In that moment, I understood that real power comes from taking radical responsibility for my own happiness. Validation must come from within.

Looking back, I've lived a life rich in experiences—successful businesses, money, beautiful homes, good relationships with family and friends. Yet, none of these external accomplishments ever brought me the deep sense of peace, happiness, and bliss I feel now. Why? Because I was never there for myself. I sought validation from the outside, constantly doubting my self-worth and giving away my power.

Now, I won't let that happen again. Believing in one's self-worth isn't always easy, especially in a world of high expectations and demands. But I've learned that it's essential to live by my own rules and truth, not someone else's.

I continue to explore the meaning of life, digging deeper into the layers of my own existence. When I rediscovered my Inner Wisdom, I found answers to two important questions:

1. *How do I recognize and remove self-sabotaging beliefs?*
2. *How do I balance the polarities within me—materialism and spirituality, femininity and masculinity—without allowing duality to pull me apart?*

Today, I am connected to the flow of life without resistance. I give myself the spaciousness I need to live fully, and I allow the creative force of life to flow through me. I have become a lover of life—embracing the bad, the beautiful, and the ugly.

I am still single, but now I have an inner peace, rooted in knowing my worth. I nurture my inner wisdom daily and have become both stronger and softer as a woman.

Through my work with women, I've come to realize that we have forgotten how to love—both ourselves and others. We are so preoccupied with fulfilling expectations that we no longer live our own dreams or speak our own truths. We must stop living in the shadows, conforming to the life others expect of us.

It's not about fighting for equal rights anymore. It's about asking why we, as women, allow ourselves to be suppressed, why we continue to self-sabotage, and why we cling to limiting beliefs.

Are you ready to let go of those beliefs and reclaim your power? I had to make the choice, and so can you.

FOOTNOTE:

In 2003, feeling both curious and frustrated about my love life, I sought out past life regression therapy in the hopes of uncovering the reasons behind why men kept leaving me. Through the therapy session, the therapist delved deep into my past life, revealing that I was a wealthy and arrogant Kungfu master who callously used and mistreated women. It was a shocking revelation that shed light on my karmic journey, indicating that I am meant to fully experience the physical and emotional pain I once inflicted upon others. This experience has provided me with a profound understanding of the consequences of my past actions and the importance of empathy and compassion in my present life.

CHAPTER 10

Healing of Self and DIY Healing

Written on 10th March 2023 – Edited 6th September 2024

I have come to understand healing through my heart, but I needed to understand it with my mind so I could clearly express it in words for my courses and workshops. I constantly ask my soul for guidance when writing.

At the most basic level, I believe we are all here on Earth in this incarnation to embrace and transmute all discordant, unloving energies within ourselves. Healing is about integrating all aspects of ourselves and, in doing so, clearing the remnants of unhealed energies from both our physical and non-physical lives.

When we resist any part of life, we resist healing. If there's a block in one direction, there's a block in every direction. Ultimately, every life challenge offers us the opportunity to embrace what we have resisted. Every challenge is healed the same way: through the realization of the power of our gratitude, words, and actions.

Reflect: Are there challenges in your life that you have been resisting? What might happen if you embraced them instead?

Our experience of life is not determined solely by our pre-birth plan but by how we respond to it. In every moment, our thoughts, words, and actions shape our experiences—and potentially our healing. When I realized that I had planned my life, I could see the deeper meaning and purpose behind everything that had happened. It became much easier to think, speak, and act with love, even in difficult times.

In my own experience, when I respond to life with love, my resistance turns into acceptance. That acceptance then grows into receptivity, and eventually, this receptivity leads to a full embrace of life. This embrace transforms into gratitude for the experiences that open our hearts and expand us as souls.

What is Healing?

Healing is reconnecting with our inner light—our true self that knows and understands. Whether it's psychological, emotional, or physical, healing occurs when we reconnect to this inner light, and that connection has a healing effect on all layers of the self: emotional, physical, and mental.

As a healer, I create an energy space that enables others to reconnect to their inner light—the part of them that knows and understands. I offer this space because I have made that connection within myself, having faced and worked through my own deep emotional challenges. Though many healers, myself included, are still on their own personal growth journeys, parts of their energy field become clear enough to have a healing effect on others.

DIY Healing Tip: One simple way to reconnect to your inner light is to spend five minutes each morning in stillness. During this time, ask yourself: *"What part of me needs love and attention today?"* Allow your intuition to guide you toward healing.

Personal Healing Experiences

Here are some specific examples of healing from March and April 2023, which were two turbulent months in my life:

1. **The Grand Re-organization and Trying to Buy a Piece of Land to Grow Medicinal Plants**

   Karen McMullen, one of my mentors, wrote a channeled book titled *Alchemy of Consciousness*, in which God/The Beloved speaks about *The Grand Re-organization* and the shift away from systems of dominance. Inspired by this, I decided to buy a piece of land to grow herbs and medicinal plants.

To fund the project, I planned to sell a small flat that I was renting out. However, the buyer pulled out at the last minute, and despite my attempts to borrow money, I couldn't raise the funds. My pride was dented, but fortunately, my son helped me get out of the purchase contract without a penalty.

Lesson: This experience made me aware of how easily self-importance and greed can creep in when we focus too much on material goals. It reminded me to listen to the true messages of my heart rather than getting caught up in the pursuit of wealth.

2. **Planning My 78th Birthday Gathering in Porto, Portugal**

   Around this time, two of my financial investment platforms collapsed, and I lost the money I had saved for the gathering. The sale of my flat also fell through. Faced with these challenges, I decided to rent out rooms in my flat through Airbnb. To my surprise, this venture was a success, and I was able to pay for the trip as planned for my children and grandchildren.

Lesson: This experience taught me the importance of flexibility and adaptability. Downsizing and renting out my flat was not a loss of face but a practical solution. By embracing change rather than resisting it, I was able to find a path forward.

3. **Family Conflict: Exclusion from My Brother-in-law's 60th Birthday Celebration**

   When I learned that my eldest daughter was invited to my brother-in-law's birthday but I was excluded, I was initially calm. However, after my sister confirmed that our other sister had refused to invite me despite her pleas, I felt deeply hurt and betrayed. To cope with these emotions, I used the Full Court of Atonement process and practiced forgiveness for myself and my sisters.

Lesson: This situation brought up feelings of resentment, regret, and jealousy, but it ultimately became a lesson in self-acceptance and self-love. I realized that healing often requires us to release hidden hostilities and trust the greater flow of life.

4. **Deceived by an Impostor Posing as My Own Daughter**

   I received an SMS from someone claiming to be my daughter, asking for money to buy a phone. The message tugged at my heartstrings, and without hesitation, I sent the money. It was only two days later that I realized I had been scammed. The feeling of betrayal and foolishness was overwhelming. However, my son helped me put it in perspective by saying, "It's just like paying ten parking fines."

Lesson: This incident prompted me to question my lack of suspicion. Was my eagerness to raise money for the land and the holiday clouding my judgment? I pondered which aspect of my unconscious needed to be revealed and transformed. What part of my karma was I meant to balance? These questions still linger, but the experience served as a powerful reminder not to rush into help without careful consideration. It reinforced the need to continually work on developing and maintaining healthy boundaries and ensuring my actions are in line with my higher purpose.

It takes discipline to practice self-examination and prioritize the healing process, especially when it comes to DIY self-healing. However, it is essential for our growth and a vital aspect of Self-Mastery and Self-Love.

To support others in their healing journey, I've created a free PDF that outlines the three energy techniques I currently use. These simple yet powerful tools can help you enhance your self-healing practice. Whether you are new to energy work or experienced in it, the PDF provides step-by-step guidance to integrate these techniques into your daily life.

In 2020, I also wrote a book titled *DIY Self-healing Using SRT, The Subconscious Release Technique*, which remains the quickest and least expensive way to energetically move from fear to health, financial well-being, inner peace, and harmony.

Healing is a lifelong journey, and embracing it is a powerful way to live an examined and fulfilled life.

CHAPTER 11

My Siblings – The Conflicts & The Joys

Written on: 26th March 2023 and continued 15th September 2024

We are four sisters—myself, Gladys, Linda, Lulu, and Lillian, the youngest. The memories of our childhood still shine vividly in my mind. One that stands out is how my mother dressed Lulu in boy's clothes until she started school. We all attended a convent school, where, for reasons unknown, Linda was always the nuns' favorite.

Our childhood on Bakri Estate, where our father was the manager, was filled with adventures. The convent school was eight miles away, and I still remember the ramshackle taxi that drove us to and from school. Our lives were lively, with parties, and we were surrounded by boys—especially Linda, who was particularly popular.

We fought often, as sisters do, but we were all equally afraid of our father's silence. There was one time, when we were very young, that sticks in my memory: we were hopping up and down on the wooden floor, causing my father's hi-fi needle to skip. He came to us and gave each of us a slap on the face. It was the only time I recall my father ever hitting me—an experience in stark contrast to my mother, who beat us all when we didn't meet her expectations.

We grew up on the rubber estate, surrounded by cobra snakes and otters, thanks to my father's passion for poultry and fish farming. His interest in small aquarium fish also meant we spent many days by streams, catching freshwater fish. Looking back, our childhood seemed happy and normal.

Moving in Different Directions

As we grew older, each of us went our separate ways. Three out of the four of us married non-Chinese men, something I still ponder over today. We saw one another during family gatherings, especially while my parents were alive. The last time all four sisters were together was in September 2017, when Linda celebrated her 70th birthday—a significant moment, as it also served as a memorial for our parents.

The 60th Birthday Exclusion

In March 2023, I was dealing with the stress of raising money to buy a small piece of land. Around that time, I learned that I had been excluded from my brother-in-law Patrick's 60th birthday celebration. When Lillian invited me to London to spend time with her and Linda after the party, I was initially thrilled at the prospect of reconnecting with two of my sisters.

However, when Linda told me that she couldn't persuade Lulu to include me in the celebration, it hit me hard. Her words triggered feelings of rejection and a flood of memories of past conflicts with Lulu. It wasn't just about the birthday—it was the deeper emotional pain of not being wanted.

I was so upset that I declined Lillian's invitation to London. The fear of being rebuked by Linda, as I had been in London in 2020, added to my reluctance.

A Letter from Kenneth

Kenneth, my brother-in-law, later heard about the situation and wrote to me:

"Are you not coming to London just because of past misunderstandings, accumulated feelings, or resentment? The reason I feel strongly about this is not because anybody is right, but because Linda will not come to Europe again. Your chance of seeing her before somebody's funeral is slim. All you have to do is smile, say you love her, and give her a hug. Then, even if nothing is said, the trip would be worth it."

His words struck a chord in me. Exhausted by the constant conflicts and emotional battles with my sisters, I responded to Kenneth, expressing my frustration at being repeatedly told that I was the problem. I felt tired of the judgments, the criticism, and the passive-aggressive dynamics among us.

In response, Kenneth wrote:

"Sad you are exhausted, but like everything in life, it will pass. Your energy will come back when you let go of everything and live in the present moment. Forget resentment."

His response brought tears to my eyes, but he was right. I knew I needed to let go. That day, I drew a tarot card—Rebirth. The message was clear: whatever state I was in, whether sleepy and depressed or rebellious and roaring, it would evolve if I allowed it. I was okay with not being part of Patrick's birthday celebration in France.

The Forgiveness Process

In June 2023, I worked with the Full Court of Atonement energy process, seeking answers. I wanted to understand why Lulu was so angry with me. What had I done to deserve her rejection?

I didn't receive an invitation to the birthday party, but I did receive photos of the event, including pictures of my daughter Jo and my granddaughter Jade. The images triggered a painful reaction in me, and I knew I had to address the negative energy I was sending out regarding my sisters.

Instead of calling them, I followed an impulse to write them a letter, which I sent on June 19, 2023:

Dear Sisters,

I trust you all had a joyful time celebrating Patrick's birthday. While I wasn't there, I've been reflecting deeply on the dynamics between us.

Lulu, I've sensed your coldness for years, especially since Papa's passing in 2007, and more so after Mummy's death in 2015. I had hoped our conversation over coffee at Karen's wedding in 2016 would heal the distance between us, but it didn't.

Recently, a friend introduced me to the concept of exonerating oneself. As someone who believes in reincarnation, I know I've been both a right-doer and a wrong-doer in many lifetimes. What about this one? What have I done to you, Lulu, to provoke such anger and rejection?

Through the forgiveness process, I asked for your forgiveness—not just yours, Lulu, but also Linda's and Lillian's.

I am so sorry, Linda, please forgive me for cutting you down in the past. I love you.

I am so sorry, Lulu, please forgive me for holding onto judgments. I love you.

I am so sorry, Lillian, please forgive me for any pain I caused. I love you.

With love, Gladys

Linda's Reply

Linda responded to my letter a few days later:

Dear Gladys,

I'm writing from my heart, which remains open to you as it always has been. I'm sorry if I have hurt you, but it was never intentional. Scolding doesn't mean I don't care or love you. I forgive you, just as much as you need to forgive me.

Her words gave me peace. We may still have our differences, but the act of forgiveness has brought us a step closer to healing.

I haven't received any replies from either Lulu or Lillian to my letter. Despite this, my relationship with Lulu remains friendly. She even took the time to wish me a happy 79th birthday on July 8, 2024. As for Lillian, nothing has changed. She continues to be my clever little sister, leading a fulfilling life in London.

Conclusion: From Conflict to Peace

On 15th Sept.2024, as I contemplated Gene Key #6—moving from conflict to peace through diplomacy—I realized that my soul contract with my sisters is to teach me inner peace. These conflicts are here to challenge me, to push me toward a deeper understanding of myself and my relationship with my family.

I'm grateful for the sisters I have, despite the conflicts. The journey hasn't been easy, but the lessons have been invaluable.

CHAPTER 12

Popo, My Grandmother, Poverty, Humiliation & Psychic Connection

Written 4th May 2023

Today, while re-reading *Alchemy of Consciousness*, I saw Karen McMullen's reflection on her fear of becoming a "bag lady." That resonated deeply with me, pulling me back to the roots of my fear of poverty. I've carried it for as long as I can remember, and it traces back to my grandmother, Popo.

Popo, whom I remember today with a mixture of kindness and sadness, lived in a small but immaculate room on Kiong Sek Road in Singapore's Chinatown. The journey to her home, however, was something I dreaded. There were dark, narrow stairs and, worse, the presence of a severely handicapped woman, tied in chains, who sat tearing newspapers into tiny bits. Sometimes she screamed. Sometimes she sat in silence. Always, it was unsettling. The fear, the discomfort, was palpable.

Popo was my mother's mother, and though her surroundings were bleak, she carried herself with a grace and dignity that still stands out in my memory. Yet, the memory of her home is not a pleasant one. She passed away at the age of 75 in a nursing home. Strangely, I didn't attend her funeral, and I still don't know why.

What stands out most about Popo is the psychic connection I felt with her—a connection that seemed to stretch across generations, as if it reached from her to my sister Lulu and me. This connection has always intrigued me, but I have never fully understood it.

Popo lived with us for a time at Jalan Ibrahim, Muar. She would tell us stories about a witch named Tam Tam Hem, stories that filled our young minds with wonder and fear. I also remember how she would chase after Lulu, who was then dressed as a boy, trying to get her to eat. Later, when we moved to Bakri Estate, Popo came with us again, but things were different this time. Papa forbade her from burning joss sticks—a small but deeply meaningful ritual for her. That was the final straw. Popo left Bakri and went to Penang.

I sometimes wonder what brought her to Singapore. Did she flee hardship in China? Or did she come seeking a better future? Did she run away from her mother-in-law? As a businesswoman, she was resourceful and resilient. She first owned a kelong, a traditional Malay fish trap, but she lost that business after an adopted son betrayed her. Later, she became a successful butcher, known for her precise skill in cutting meat. But I also remember her selling vegetables by the roadside, a humbling sight for someone who had once been so much more.

And yet, her dignity remained. I will never forget one thing she often said: *"Leh Yu Sek Cho Yun"—You must know how to be truly human*. Those words echo in my mind even today and may have influenced me sub-consciously to the extent that I coach others to know what it is to be a whole human being, warts and all.

The Psychic Connection

For as long as I can remember, I've sensed a psychic connection between Popo, Lulu, and myself. But I've never been able to understand it fully. Did we share a past life? It feels as though we did. Two particular incidents still weigh on me:

1. The first was when Papa was on his way to a heart operation. While we were at the Johore Causeway, I made a casual remark that distracted Mama, causing her to miss the correct turn into Singapore. Lulu turned to me with characteristic sharpness and said, "You always talk too much." Her words stung, and I cried for hours. I couldn't stop.

2. The second happened during a trip to India with my sister Linda. We were visiting the place where Buddha achieved enlightenment. One evening, while discussing Lulu's coldness toward me, I began to cry again, the emotions overwhelming me once more.

These moments have they left me with a lingering question: How do I release the psychic debris between us? How do I clear the space between myself and my grandmother or between myself and Lulu? My spirit guides have told me that I cannot force this. But I can clear my energy by making peace with them as they are—by finding the lessons I was meant to learn from our interactions.

This is not easy. But I know that, in doing so, I can ensure that my energy is clear. I can ensure that I harbor no ill will or ill intent toward them.

Finding Peace

I've been told that both Lulu and Popo will sense this shift if they ever come into contact with my energy again. When my own space is clear and peaceful, I can uplift them—even if they do not fully understand or want it.

Can this truly be so? I've often been told that I am an old soul, and perhaps this is part of my role in this lifetime—to clear this psychic debris, to find peace where once there was conflict. Whether or not I ever fully understand the depth of our connection, I now know that my task is to live in peace with it, to release the burdens that are no longer mine to carry.

In healing myself, I am healing them. And in healing them, I am healing the generations to come.

Conclusion

True healing begins within. We cannot force others to meet us on the same path, but we can clear our energy, make peace with our experiences, and release the burdens of the past. In doing so, we free ourselves—and perhaps, by the grace of the universe, we also free those we love.

CHAPTER 13

My Father, His Father—Humiliation & Reconciliation

Written on 29th March 2023

This morning, during my contemplation, I felt a deep impulse to work on *Healing the Unspoken Collateral Damage of World War II*. The negative emotions I encountered were intense. When I worked on **contempt**, I sensed the imprint came from my mother. But it was when I focused on **humiliation** that I felt something even deeper—something connected to my father.

As I delved into this energy, I realized it didn't stop with my father. It led me back to *his* father, my paternal grandfather. He was taken by the Japanese as a prisoner-of-war, and no one knew what became of him. But today, through the Full Court of Atonement, I sensed the truth—he was beheaded. The weight of that revelation shook me.

With prayers, I began my ritual of release:

I, Lian Henriksen, place myself, Gladys Chew Geok Lian Henriksen, into a Full Court of Atonement with all levels of consciousness that feel humiliation. I ask to analyze my timeline and resolve any and all reasons for this feeling of humiliation, at its point of origin. I ask for an amenable dissolution of this energy. I forbid this energy further access to my body, my energy fields, and my timeline. Go away. Go away.

As I recited the prayer, I was drawn back to an experience in 2007, shortly after my father passed away. I had been in Los Angeles with

Bruce, my partner at the time. He suggested I meet a shamanic priestess named Mataji. Though I can't recall all the details of the conversation, one thing remains clear—Mataji instructed me to perform a ritual for my father, who had died on the 14th of February that year.

The ritual involved finding rich soil, placing it in a container that could float on water, and releasing it into the Pacific Ocean to let it drift toward Japan. This, she said, would bring peace to my father's spirit. Bruce and I set out immediately after the meeting to find the materials. Mataji insisted the container not be plastic, so I chose a simple metal foil tray.

As we drove through the countryside in search of the perfect spot, something unusual happened. We noticed a large number of hawks—or perhaps falcons—circling in the sky. Bruce remarked how strange it was to see so many at once. I remember feeling deeply moved by the sight, though I didn't fully understand why at the time. There was something transcendent about it, a message I couldn't yet grasp.

I stepped out of the van, collected the soil, and we drove to the Pacific Ocean. There, I let the soil float away in the tray, watching it disappear into the vastness of the water. As it drifted toward Japan, I felt a mixture of sadness and relief. I hoped, as Mataji had promised, that this would bring peace to my father.

As I reflect on this ritual today, two memories come to mind. The first is of my maternal grandfather, who lost his sanity during the war. My mother was told by her mother—my grandmother—how he would cook many pots of rice and pour it into the drains to feed the souls of the dead. My grandmother, Popo, never knew where he went or whether he died. The second memory is of my father's final moments.

My Father's Struggle

My father's death was not peaceful. He struggled—*literally* clawing his way through something unseen. Watching him in those final hours was heartbreaking. The doctors offered conflicting advice on how to ease his suffering. One recommended giving him water; the other advised against it. In the end, I trusted my instinct and kept his mouth moist with a cotton bud, hoping it might bring him some small comfort.

My father never truly recovered from the trauma of World War II. The war left him spiritually wounded. Shortly after the war, he left the Protestant church, saying, "I cannot believe in a God who allows men to be so cruel." His faith wavered for much of his life, but I always sensed the spiritual bothered him deeply. Strangely, when he was about 70 years old, he got baptized again, as if seeking a reconciliation with the divine that he had rejected for so long.

He rarely spoke of his family, but on the rare occasions that he did, his words revealed the depth of his pain. He once mentioned his younger sister, saying, "Poor Nancy, she has suffered so much." And just before he died, he spoke of his mother, adding only, "She had a hard life." It was as if these moments of quiet reflection revealed more than years of silence could.

As my cousin recently reminded me, "Your father was a very stern man when he was young." That sternness, I now realize, was a reflection of the deep hurt and humiliation he carried, a pain shaped by the war and the family losses he never truly reconciled.

Reconciling the Past

My father's death marked the end of a man who never fully healed from the spiritual and emotional scars of war. The hatred he harbored for the Japanese, and the humiliation that accompanied it, stayed with him until his last breath. That hatred, that sense of betrayal by both humanity and the divine, shaped much of who he was.

In my contemplation today, I realize that the ritual wasn't just about healing my father. It was about healing the legacy of humiliation that has echoed through our family. By acknowledging it, by facing it, and by performing these acts of reconciliation, I hope that the energy of that humiliation no longer has power over us.

As I conclude this chapter, I find myself still wondering—has my father found peace? Has the pain of his father's death and the scars of war finally been lifted from his soul?

CHAPTER 14

My Life with My Father as I Recall

Written on 18th Sept. 2024

This morning, although my intention was to work on my 78th birthday reflections, I felt a calling to write about my father's life and his attitude towards being Chinese, as well as his complex relationship with Communist China.

My father was born on June 17, 1918, and passed away on February 14, 2007. He was the eldest of nine children, and his father, my grandfather, worked as a clerk in a law firm. The family home, one of the finest on Bukit Timah, Singapore, was a large, beautiful residence. I still have many photos of it and can vividly recall its rambutan trees, as well as moments with Uncle David and Aunty Nancy dancing. One childhood memory that stands out is when I locked myself in the bathroom, panicking until Uncle David came to my rescue. The fear and confusion of that moment stayed with me for years.

My father was a qualified agriculturist, having graduated from Serdang Agriculture College in Kuala Lumpur. His career began as a valuer for The Overseas Chinese Bank in Singapore. He married my mother in 1944, during the height of the war, and they fled to Pulau Batam to escape the worst of the fighting. It was there that my father grew vegetables, chilies, and raised pigs to feed the family, as well as his siblings. Before the war ended, he was transferred to Kota Tinggi.

I remember hearing stories about how he would mislead the Japanese soldiers and about the gruesome sight of beheaded heads hanging from the Kota Tinggi bridge. The war years left deep scars on him. My sister, Linda, was born in 1947 in Batu Pahat, and by 1950, we had moved to Muar, where my father became the manager of Bakri Estate, a rubber plantation owned by Lee Plantations.

Our home in Muar was a traditional Malay house on stilts, with a long, dark corridor running through the center of it. The kitchen and dining area were at the back, on the ground floor. One vivid memory I have is of my mother skinning iguanas for soup because my sister suffered from asthma. I also recall the one dark indoor bathroom, which had a large brick water container, and the outdoor toilet, where a man would come and collect the waste. Life was simple and, in many ways, it felt adventurous.

What was not so simple were my father's moods. He could be warm, but when he was in a bad mood, he resorted to "Dead Silence." My siblings and I were scared stiff of him during these times, especially at dinner. The silence was almost oppressive, and even the smallest mistake or word out of place felt dangerous. I remember trying to avoid his gaze, afraid of doing or saying something that might break the quiet in the wrong way. This side of him made him seem larger than life, a figure both powerful and unreachable. It left an indelible mark on how we interacted with him, always treading carefully around his moods.

My father once came home with a flashy Studebaker car after receiving his first bonus, but his boss told him to return it. Though I can't remember whether he exchanged it for a Volvo or Rover, I do recall his deep excitement and later, his quiet acceptance of his boss's order. It was moments like these that demonstrated his internal conflict—between wanting to enjoy the fruits of his labor and adhering to the expectations placed upon him.

As for the war against the Malaysian Communist Party, it is worth noting that this was a completely separate struggle from the Japanese occupation. After the war, my father became involved in the fight against communist insurgents who had pledged their loyalty to Communist China. Planters like my father were prime targets, especially around paydays when ambushes were common. His position as an estate manager made him a target, and it became routine for our home to be surrounded by barbed wire and guarded 24/7 by armed security. A tall lookout post was also constructed nearby to detect any approaching threats.

There was even a story my father once told me, in a rare reflective moment, about a communist woman who threw a hand grenade at him. He shot and killed her, only to discover later that she was pregnant. This haunted him deeply, as he carried the weight of that act for the rest of his life. He never visited China, partly out of fear that he was still a target of the Chinese Communist Party.

The end of the communist emergency meant our family could move to Bakri Estate, where life took on a more peaceful rhythm. My father invested his energy into farming freshwater fish, including carp, and raising poultry. These were wonderful years, filled with boating, swimming, and hunting pigeons. The old mining pond in front of the house was a place of endless fun for my siblings and me. My 21st birthday party was held there, and so was the wedding dinner for my first marriage. It was a place that held many fond memories, where life felt simple and joyful, despite the underlying tensions we all navigated.

It's clear that my father carried a lot of inner struggles with him throughout his life. He had to step up as the head of the family of 9 siblings after losing both his parents during the 2nd World War. There are three remarks he made that have stayed with me. The first was about leaving James, his brother, to handle their father's estate, which resulted in the siblings being left with nothing. When his youngest sister, Nancy, fell gravely ill, he showed his emotions and simply said, "Poor Nancy, she has suffered so much." The last of the three memories came just before he died, when he spoke of his mother, saying, "My mother had a hard life. She tried making money playing tontine." These statements revealed a profound, unspoken pain that he rarely shared with others.

In the 35 years we lived at Bakri Estate, my father thrived in his farming pursuits, though his disagreements with his bosses about pension payments eventually led him to retire early.

He moved to Jalan Waspada in Johore Bahru. He spent much of his time on building huge kites which he flew in kite flying meets all over the world. Jalan Waspada was the family home for us siblings and our children. My parent's diamond wedding anniversary was held here. My father lived there until his death on February 14, 2007.

He was a man of contradictions, shaped by war, loss, and responsibility. His life left a lasting imprint on me.

As I reflect on his life, one particular letter he wrote to me in 1983 stands out. It captures both his stern nature and his deep, albeit quiet, love for his family:

My dear Gladys and Bjorn,

We have our air tickets and will be leaving Singapore by Pan Am Flight No.7 at 7:15 am on December 6th. We are joyously looking forward to seeing all of you, most of all Kim. We want to share in the happiness the little fellow is giving you both.

Today is the day we shall have Kenneth and Jo-Ann stay with us for a few days. I shall make this event the turning point of our relationship with Boston and Katherine. There is no other choice. I think when I build up the trust Boston has in me to the point where he knows I am not trying to steal the kids' affection from him, all should be well! The pity of it all is that he had to take it out on the kids—especially Kenneth. I shall never be able to live in peace with myself if I just abandon them to their misfortune. Life won't be worth a penny if I did.

With peace and love,

Papa

As I re-read his words, I am reminded of the complex man he was—firm in his beliefs, but deeply committed to his family. His life shaped mine in ways I am only now beginning to fully understand.

CHAPTER 15

My Relationship to Money

Written on: 22nd March 2023

My Financial Background

At one point in my life, I was a highly successful businesswoman, one of the most well-paid women in Denmark from 1995 to 2003. Then came a time when I was as poor as a church mouse. After losing my firm, I was declared personally bankrupt. Adjusting to a life of financial hardship was one of the most challenging experiences of my life. The court case against me dragged on for ten years because my business partner's lawyer believed I had hidden wealth in offshore accounts. He spent a decade digging into my private life, looking for fortunes that simply didn't exist.

Instead of relying on social assistance, I chose to earn a living by caring for the elderly, a path I hadn't imagined for myself but one that turned out to be unexpectedly rewarding. When I turned 65, I stopped working as a caregiver, having built a modest but sufficient private pension. Yet, I faced another setback when the American company, owned by my partner then, I had invested in went bust during the 2008 financial crisis. For a while, I supported myself as an Ayurvedic yoga masseur.

In 2015, I inherited money from my parents and decided to invest in learning how to build wealth. In 2016, I met JT Foxx, who claims to be The World's No.1 Wealth Coach. He encouraged me to strive for millionaire status. I was coached by one of his associates and later interviewed by him on stage at Tycoons of Wealth in Johannesburg, South Africa. However, the experience left me feeling disillusioned, and I ended up $20,000 poorer. I also spent a significant sum of money learning about property ownership in the UK, but this venture was unsuccessful due to the arrival of COVID-19. I then turned to investing in cryptocurrency, which also turned out to be a disaster. What have been my lessons to these experiences? What opportunities of growth have they provided me?

My Current Relationship with Money

Today, my relationship with money is more aligned with the values I hold dear—simplicity, authenticity, and spiritual surrender. My financial decisions now reflect a deeper alignment with my spiritual path.

Every morning in my stillness, I offer this prayer:

Dearest Beloved,

You say my relationship with money—how I give and receive—is a perfect or near-perfect gauge of my proximity to You. You ask me to perfect my relationship with money as I perfect my relationship with You. I ask: How can I best serve You? And You respond by asking me to live a simple life, free of ambitions to do big or impressive things. You ask me to be an image of love, contentment, peace, purity, harmony, and essential harmlessness in my very being.

Recently, I considered selling my flat at Hillerødgade to purchase a small piece of land for growing food and medicinal plants. I've worked hard toward this goal, but I continue to seek Your guidance on whether this decision aligns with Your will.

To support this, I performed a Full Court of Atonement with all levels of my consciousness, asking for the resolution of any blockages related to the sale of Hillerødgade. I asked to analyze my timeline, resolve the points of origin of any blocks, and dissolve them in the most benevolent way. I forbid any further energy blockage from affecting my body, my timeline, or my energy field, and I ask for the most favorable outcome.

What is Living a Simple Life?

The answer that continues to come to me is clear:

- **Growing food and medicinal teas** free from insecticides, pesticides, and fungicides.
- **Nurturing happy relationships** with my family and a few close friends.
- **Living with few, but high-quality clothes** that truly serve me.
- **Maintaining a healthy body.**
- **Achieving authentic financial freedom** by living in alignment with my true needs, not the excesses of society.

This is how I feel I can serve my part in the evolutionary dance. The purpose and deeper meaning of my life are to align myself with the Beloved's will and to shine from that essence. From this alignment, I will experience the perfect circumstances for the Beloved's will to be fulfilled through me. I must let go, trust, and surrender. I must take each step in the now—one step at a time, moment by moment.

I want to be a conscious conduit for the Beloved's will.

The Full Court of Atonement Money Call that I continue to use from time to time and as often as I can remember to do so:

I place myself, Lian Henriksen and the entirety of my family lineages into a Full Court of Atonement with money, bills and paying taxes. I ask them to correct all conflicts between us at their point of origin. I ask to resolve any-and-all-need for retaliation, revenge or restitution. I ask us all to repent. I ask us all to redeem ourselves and make amends. I ask myself to create peace with myself with all money issues.

Postscript – Written on 19th September 2024

I am now considering selling my small flat again—but this time, to raise funds for a family reunion on my 80th birthday in 2024. It feels like this, too, is part of the greater plan unfolding.

CHAPTER 16

My 78th Birthday – Gathering of The Clan at Porto, Portugal

Written on 14th July 2023 and 16th July 2023

As I approached my 78th birthday, I found myself reflecting deeply on the relationships within my family. Watching my grandchildren, Josephine and Anton, after their parents' recent divorce, I couldn't help but notice a change in their behavior. They seemed less confident, less sure of themselves. It made me reflect on how the dynamics between parents and children ripple through generations, and how changes in relationships, no matter how well-intentioned, can leave lasting marks.

This reflection on my grandchildren's experiences also brought me back to my journey, reminding me of something I read in Gene Key 23: Complexity > Simplicity > Quintessence. Richard Rudd writes about how most people don't design their lives intelligently and instead react to event after event. By the time they reach 40, their lives have become so complex that it takes the rest of their years to regain simplicity.

At 78, I now see myself at a point of returning to simplicity. After so many relationship breakdowns and challenges, I advocate for the simplicity of commitment: to stay in a relationship and use the hard times as opportunities for transformation. Blundering in and out of relationships leaves behind extraordinary debris—divorce proceedings, divided children, debts, and lifelong resentments. Complexity upon complexity.

Designing one's life with intention takes discipline. It requires care and mindfulness. As I prepared for the family gathering in Porto, Portugal, I asked for divine guidance. I wanted to be present, centered, and at peace with myself, especially when surrounded by my children and grandchildren. I felt incredibly blessed to have this opportunity to bring everyone together for a week, and I wanted to navigate the experience with grace and wisdom.

In the lead-up to the gathering, I performed the Full Court of Atonement (FCOA) process, consistently asking for divine guidance. My prayer was simple: that kindness would be the intention of all of us. The first few days were joyful. On my birthday, I received a beautiful necklace with four semi-precious stones from my four children. We bonded over a 1,000-piece jigsaw puzzle, a gift from my daughter-in-law. But on the fourth day, a conflict erupted. My son accused me of taking sides – taking the side of my daughter and not remain in a neutral energy.

In the aftermath, I turned inward, silently asking for forgiveness and working through decrees to heal the energy between us. I focused on centering myself in the healing art of reconciliation—not just with my children, but with all the family connections that came before and after us. I needed to reconcile with my children, their partners, my ancestors, and even the parents of my children's in-laws. It was a spiritual process of deepening peace within me, knowing that healing one relationship helps heal many others across time.

We left our holiday home, *Trebid Ouo-Casa de Campo Rua Funda da Aldeira*, on July 13, 2023. As we packed the completed jigsaw of the moon, I knew I still had internal work to do. The physical act of putting the pieces together felt symbolic of my emotional and spiritual work: piecing together fractured relationships, finding a way to mend them, and holding onto hope for wholeness.

Upon returning home, I wrote a letter to my children and their partners:

Dear Kenneth and Julie, JoAnn & Paolo, Kim and Victoria, Karen and Dennis,

Once again, thank you for spending your time, energy, and money to be present at my birthday reunion. It was a joy to see you all bonding, especially with my grandchildren. But my greatest joy was witnessing the growing intimacy between you four as siblings and with your partners.

That said, I must confess I overestimated my ability to transport the fully completed 1,000-piece moon jigsaw. The tape around the cardboard burst open on the bus ride home. Kenneth, I'm sorry I couldn't find a baggage-wrapping machine at the Porto airport.

With the job incomplete, I spent today energetically centering myself in reconciliation. I worked through a series of decrees to help heal and strengthen the bonds between us all. I hope you feel the effects of this energy work, and if any of you need the decrees, just let me know.

As for the jigsaw puzzle, I haven't dared open the package to see the damage. It occurred to me that perhaps we should all open it together. What do you think, Kim and Victoria? We could repair the missing pieces using *Kintsugi*, the Japanese art of mending with gold or silver. It's a philosophy that teaches us to treat breakage as part of the object's history, rather than something to hide. Let me know what you think.

Here is a photo of the stones on the cork bark from Porto, representing me and my six grandchildren. Guess which stone represents which grandchild?

Love,

Your mother & mother-in-law

Only Kenneth and Julie responded to this letter, but I continued my inner work. I knew I had to forgive myself for not navigating the gathering as smoothly as I had hoped. I worked with the following decrees:

I heal all the wounds I have inflicted or have been held responsible for, in all moments.

I let go of the grip I hold onto those I have judged, in all moments.

I restore all lifetimes as a healer, in all moments.

I resolve all differences more amicably, in all moments.

I breathe new life into my inner being and fill the cracks with the golden light of compassion and self-forgiveness.

I am Kintsugi-ed now.

After reflecting on Gene Key #62, I embraced the beauty of my mistakes. There is great power in seeing the cracks and mending them with love. I know that the only real influence I have in this universe is my presence, fully and authentically, in each moment.

Three months passed before I saw Kim and his family again. Despite the conflict, I have no regrets about holding the gathering. It served its purpose—to bring us together, to allow us to bond, and to face the challenges as they came. I'm already planning another reunion for my 80th birthday. The energy work will continue, but this time, with more understanding and more grace.

CHAPTER 17

Aftermath of the Birthday Gathering: Regret, Reconciliation & Forgiveness

Written on 17th July 2023 & 5th August 2023

My 78th birthday was meant to be a time of reunion, healing, and celebration—a time to bring my children, their partners, and my grandchildren together. After years of navigating the complex web of family dynamics, this was my chance to witness the growth and closeness that had been built among them. But, as with all families, old wounds can resurface, and conflicts often arise when least expected.

I gathered everyone in Porto, Portugal, in July 2023, filled with hope. But as the days passed, the tension grew, and conflict eventually erupted. I found myself caught off guard and overwhelmed by the sudden shift in energy.

My Regret

At the birthday circle, after thanking my children for their gifts, I felt compelled to share something I had long carried with me. With a heart full of emotion, I told them that my one regret in life was abandoning my first two children.

Back in 1979, before I left for China and changed my citizenship from Malaysian to Danish, I hadn't secured a watertight custody agreement with their father. I initially had custody of Ken and Jo, but when their father discovered I was going to be with another man—the father of my third and fourth children—he sued me for adultery, which cost me my right to custody. Even visitation rights were given up, as my children were punished after each visit. I didn't see them for eight long years.

This regret has lingered within me, affecting how I navigate every family relationship. But I realize now that the past cannot be undone. It can only be reconciled within myself.

Conflict with Kim

As the family gathered in Porto, there was a sense of celebration. We were together, sharing meals, and enjoying the beautiful setting. But tensions were simmering below the surface. On the fourth day, a conflict arose between my son Kim and me. It was unexpected and deeply painful. Kim accused me of taking sides in a disagreement between his partner Victoria and my daughter Karen.

It was an uncomfortable situation, and in my frustration, I lashed out. Later, Kim messaged me, explaining how hurtful my actions had been toward Victoria, who was pregnant at the time. He told me I hadn't remained neutral, that I had taken sides, and had yelled at them, which left him and Victoria feeling unsupported.

This conflict cut deep. I've always tried to stay neutral, to act as a mediator, but I failed. I knew I had to take responsibility for my actions, so I apologized to Kim and Victoria. But even after my apology, the uneasy feeling lingered. I felt as though I hadn't truly resolved the hurt. The conflict was a mirror, reflecting my unhealed wounds.

My Process of Reconciliation

After the trip, I knew I had to work on healing the rift, not just with Kim, but with myself. I turned to the spiritual tools that have always guided me—the Full Court of Atonement (FCOA) and the healing decrees. I knew that reconciliation had to come from within, and I couldn't force anyone else to heal their wounds. But I could heal mine. As I worked through the FCOA, I realized that forgiveness was not a one-time act; it was a process.

I used the following decrees to help center myself:

- I help myself become centered and empowered in the healing art of reconciliation, in all moments.
- I am centered and empowered in the healing art of reconciliation with all my children in all moments.
- I am centered and empowered in the healing art of reconciliation with the partners of my children in all moments.

These decrees brought me a sense of peace, though the process wasn't easy. Forgiveness and reconciliation are ongoing practices, and they demand patience.

The Symbolism of the Puzzle and the Moon

During the trip, my daughter-in-law Victoria gifted me a 1,000-piece jigsaw puzzle of the moon. It was meant to be a bonding experience for the family, and together we completed it. However, on the return flight, the puzzle was damaged—30 pieces went missing.

At first, I was upset. The puzzle symbolized the gathering, and its completion felt significant. But as I reflected on the missing pieces, I saw the symbolism more clearly. Just like the puzzle, there are pieces of myself and my relationships that are still missing, still fragmented. But rather than seeing this as a failure, I now view it as an opportunity. The Native Americans believe that life is like a jigsaw puzzle—pieces of ourselves become lost over time, and it takes years to find and restore them.

The missing pieces are part of the journey. Perhaps I will spend the rest of my life finding and restoring those lost pieces. Maybe it will be fun. Maybe it will be hard. But I trust the process.

Forgiveness and Healing

In the aftermath of the birthday gathering, I was reminded of the importance of self-forgiveness. The conflict with Kim was a reflection of the deeper wounds within me—the fear of rejection, the need for validation, and the pain of not being fully understood. But I now know that I cannot heal anyone else's wounds. I can only heal my own.

I placed myself into a Full Court of Atonement with Kim and Victoria, asking for resolution, for forgiveness. I acknowledged that I had not forgiven them, and I asked for forgiveness in return. I worked through my anger, my pain, and finally, I found peace. The process wasn't immediate, but it was real.

After a few days, I delivered some mangoes to Kim and Victoria's home. Although invited for coffee, I didn't stay long. But before I left, my granddaughter Augusta rushed over and gave me a caterpillar as a gift. It was a small gesture, but it touched me deeply. The caterpillar, a symbol of transformation, reminded me that change is always happening. We are always evolving, always becoming something new.

Conclusion

I know now that reconciliation is not about forcing others to heal or change. It is about healing yourself, and in doing so, creating space for others to heal in their own time. The birthday gathering was not perfect, but it was a powerful opportunity for growth. The conflict with Kim, though painful, allowed me to see the parts of myself that still need healing. And as I continue to heal, I trust that my family, too, will find their own path to healing.

In the end, life is like a jigsaw puzzle—sometimes the pieces fit perfectly, and sometimes they go missing. But with time, patience, and love, the picture becomes whole again.

CHAPTER 18

Aging, Pain and Building A Legacy of Insight and Understanding

The Bedrock of Truth
Written: 14th August 2023, 26th August 2023, and 28th August 2023

The Beloved says:

"No one can harm you. The foundation of Truth—your bedrock—can absorb everything, including projections, hurtful words, and challenges. There is freedom in not only knowing this but in experiencing it: watching as what once triggered the ego passes through you, absorbed into your core. The next time something elicits an emotional reaction, try to receive those words or that news into the very center of your being—the bedrock of Truth.

Truth includes both light and darkness, all experiences and storylines. Nothing is wrong, it just is. Accepting this, without mounting a battle or revolt, dissolves the war within. This process ends conflict not only within yourself but can also help liberate others. It's a simple practice, but not easy. The layers of ego must be worn lightly, allowing you to be permeable and open. When the ego is thin, you can transform the importance of things that 'matter' to you and neutralize their emotional impact."

The Beloved emphasizes that true power lies in the ability to absorb and neutralize, to dissolve anything into the Truth. This power, however, is only accessible after working deeply with your own pain and egoic layers. It's not avoidance or emotional bypassing—it's advanced work that comes from being grounded in Truth.

Reflections on Aging

Recently, aging has made itself known to me in unmistakable ways. The removal of three teeth and awaiting implants was a reminder of the physical changes I'm experiencing. My hips ache, and incontinence has been another challenge. In these moments of discomfort, I pray for understanding and release from any disharmony surrounding the process of aging.

I ask myself, "What is the purpose of the rest of my life? What legacy do I want to leave? What contribution have I made?" The answers that come are simple yet profound: **Seek Truth. Seek Harmony. Be the Light.**

A Day of Insights

On August 27th, three important events unfolded that deepened my reflections:

1. I received a clear message from The Beloved to focus on my **legacy**.

2. I visited an exhibition by Joen Vedel about his father, Peter Petersen, which explored how Joen came to terms with the life his father lived—a mirror of the reflections I've had about my own life.

3. Over dinner with my son Kim, I encouraged him to reconcile with his father, a gesture that felt aligned with my own spiritual practice of seeking harmony.

The Legacy Path – Osho Tarot Reading

The next morning, I turned to my **Osho Tarot Cards**, using the **Celtic Cross spread** for insight on my legacy:

- **Past Lives**: The patterns of karma and unconscious behavior repeating across lifetimes are surfacing for review. This card is a wake-up call, urging me to see and understand the karmic cycles of my life.

- **Integration**: The union of opposites—eagle and swan, fire and water—speaks to the alchemy of life. Integration is the symbol of self-creation and the mystical union of opposing forces within.

- **Maturity**: True joy comes from hard work well done. I am in a solid place now, with a stable foundation beneath me.

- **Success**: The peaks and valleys of life are fleeting—this too shall pass. Celebrate the highs and the lows with equal grace.

- **Participation**: Engage with life fully, making participation a joyful lifestyle.

- **Possibilities**: Because I have grown in self-love and acceptance, new possibilities are opening to me. The world is providing what I need at exactly the right time.

- **Suppression**: I have repressed much of my vitality in the past, trying to meet expectations. The message is clear: I must find a healing outlet for the tensions that have built up.

- **Silence**: The energy of the whole universe possesses me when I am still. In silence, I am no more—only the whole exists.

- **The Source**: A reminder that infinite energy is always available to me, not through thinking or planning but through grounding, centering, and silence.
- **Breakthrough**: The ultimate message: to transform breakdowns into breakthroughs is life's greatest adventure. The chaos I have carried for lifetimes can lead to liberation, as long as I pass through the darkest night in search of the dawn.

Note added on 24th September 2024:

As I transferred this handwritten chapter, written in August 2023, to my computer today, I realized how the Osho Tarot reading had been a prelude—a warning of sorts. It foreshadowed the difficult events I would experience between September and November 2023. These months tested my resolve in unexpected ways, but in hindsight, this chapter of my life has guided me toward a deeper understanding of Truth and the legacy I wish to embody.

CHAPTER 19

My Ousting from Jenuine Healing and Forgiveness

Written on: 26th November 2023 and 17th December 2023

In late October 2023, I found myself deeply immersed in the **Jenuine Healing Community**, guided by **Jen Ward**, a world-renowned energy healer, and her partner **Marvin Schneider**, a technological expert. During one of my healing sessions with Jen, we spoke about the structure of the spiritual world and the importance of empowering ourselves to be our own gurus. It felt like a homecoming to be part of a community that shared my belief in self-empowerment and spiritual autonomy.

Inspired by this connection, I made a **Facebook post** on 26th November 2023, where I invited others to join me in a small group focused on **Awakening, Enlightenment, and Ascension**. I wrote:

"I hope to manifest 5 people to form a small group where we can talk and share personal insights on Awakening, Enlightenment, and Ascension. Will you be one of them? I have been coaching and mentoring young women on authentic financial freedom for the last five years, but I now wish to focus on exploring enlightenment and becoming whole while living in a higher state of consciousness."

I shared that my tools for personal empowerment were **The Gene Keys** by Richard Rudd and Jen Ward's **Spiritual Freedom Technique (SFT)**, and I envisioned us working together on **Zoom**, occasionally meeting in person. To my delight, six people responded positively, and I was excited about the possibilities that lay ahead.

Later that same day, I received an email from **Marvin Schneider**, expressing concern over my Facebook post. He explained that Jen had noticed a pattern where people, after becoming empowered through her sessions, would use her techniques to draw attention to themselves or form their own groups. This behavior, according to Marvin, depleted energy from **Jenuine Healing's mission** to uplift humanity. He suggested I take a break from the community, focus on deeper healing through private sessions with Jen, and canceled my subscription. His words were:

"We think it is best if you take a break from the Jenuine Healing Community and the weekly Open House events. There are several core issues that you are fighting against that are best addressed in a series of private sessions with Jen."

I was shocked. I had no intention of using Jen's teachings for personal gain, only to share what had been meaningful to me with others on similar paths. Confused and hurt, I immediately called **Connie**, my friend who had introduced me to Jen in the first place. Talking to her helped, but the emotional impact was profound.

The next morning, I woke up with a swollen left eye and debilitating pain in my left knee, making it difficult to walk without crutches. I developed a pain in my throat and whooping cough. My body seemed to be reacting physically to the emotional turmoil I was going through.

Over the following days, I sought help to release the intense emotions of anger, betrayal, and confusion. In a **Full Court of Atonement** session with **Amy Jo Ellis** on 28th November, I was chosen to share my experience. Amy helped me clear the lingering sense of betrayal that had taken hold of me, providing some relief. Yet, the healing process was far from over.

I continued working with **Connie**, using **Radical Forgiveness Worksheets** to release the layers of anger I felt. This process allowed me to gradually move through the stages of grief, from anger and confusion to acceptance. Connie's support was invaluable during this time, helping me to see the situation from a higher perspective.

On **12th December**, after ten days of physical illness and intense emotional processing, I woke up nearly pain-free. I felt a renewed sense of clarity and peace, as though something deep within me had shifted. In this moment of stillness, I received an intuitive nudge to reconnect with **The Sophia Code**, a sacred transmission I had studied deeply in 2021 but had set aside. This living transmission is designed to support the healing of our deepest wounds and to guide us toward embodying our highest potential.

Affirmation of Self-Compassion

On **17th December**, I spent time working with **Key Code 6** from **The Sophia Code** "She of A Thousand Waters, Quan Yin. As I meditated on these sacred teachings, I was reminded of the importance of holding myself with tenderness and compassion. It is from this place of self-love that true healing can occur, and I felt a deep shift within me as I practiced the following affirmation:

"I accept that I hold the golden keys to my Heaven on Earth.

I accept that I create my reality, by the power of my word.

My word is good, my heart is pure.

By the loving power of my pure word, I call forth and declare blessings of unconditional compassion for myself now."

As I spoke these words aloud, a profound sense of peace washed over me. However, I realized that a deeper healing was needed. I felt compelled to address a recurring pattern in my life—an unconscious tendency to perpetuate suffering. Like many, I often found myself trapped in cycles of pain and negativity without fully realizing it.

At this moment, I made a powerful declaration:

"By the power of my I Am Presence, I now forgive myself for every addiction to unconsciously perpetuate further suffering."

This realization was a pivotal moment for me. I recognized that, like so many humans, I had unconsciously clung to suffering as a familiar pattern. But by acknowledging this, I could begin to release it. Forgiving myself for these unconscious behaviors was the key to moving forward.

Moving Forward

As I continue my journey toward **Self-Mastery** and **Higher Consciousness**, I am learning to fully embody compassion for myself. The teachings of **The Sophia Code** and **The Gene Keys** and the techniques I've practiced have helped me to heal on deeper levels than I ever imagined. I now trust that I am fully capable of creating my reality—a reality filled with joy, love, and peace.

Through this process of self-forgiveness, I have begun to break the cycles of suffering and step into the life I am meant to live. I am empowered by the knowledge that **I hold the golden keys to my Heaven on Earth**, and by the power of my word, I can manifest a life of happiness, abundance, and unconditional love.

Each day is a step forward in embodying my **Higher Self** and living in alignment with my deepest truth. With this newfound clarity, I feel ready for whatever comes next on this sacred journey.

CHAPTER 20

Cultural Conflicts in Names

Written: 27th January 2024
I am **Gladys Chew Geok Lian Henriksen**.
My name is **Geok Lian**, but call me **Lian**.

Like many in my generation from Singapore and Malaysia, my name reflects a layered history. On my **birth certificate**, I am **Chew Geok Lian**—**Chew** as the surname, **Geok Lian** as the traditional two-part Chinese given name. Yet, my family has always called me **Gladys**, a name that was never officially registered but used affectionately by my parents.

Even as a child, I wouldn't say I liked the name **Gladys**. To me, it was a name associated with maids or servants working in the homes of the English upper class. It never felt like it belonged to me or reflected who I was. Despite that, it became the name I was known by in everyday life, which distanced me from my Chinese heritage and my given name, **Geok Lian**.

In Singapore, having an **English name** was expected, a legacy of British colonialism, and most teachers preferred it. **Gladys** became my everyday identity, making things easier, though it created a subtle disconnect from my given Chinese name.

When I first moved to **Denmark** in 1982, I continued using **Gladys**, despite my discomfort with it. It wasn't until 2003 that I decided to use only **Lian Henriksen**, a blend of my Chinese identity and my married Danish surname, which I kept after my divorce. However, this has created an interesting division. Some Danes, particularly those who knew me from earlier, still call me **Gladys**. Others, especially in formal settings like hospitals or with doctors, call me **Geok**, while more recently, many call me **Lian**.

Names and the Search for Identity

I've often wondered how my name affects my sense of self. **Who am I**, really? Is it **Gladys**, the name I disliked but used for much of my life? **Lian**, the name that connects me to my Chinese heritage and feels most aligned with who I am now? Or is it **Henriksen**, the name that ties me to my life in Denmark?

My **mother** never had an English name. In fact, she referred to herself as "a child with no name" because her family always called her **Ah Lui**, meaning "daughter." This contrasted with my **father**, who never had a **Chinese name**—he only had an English name. My experience sits between these two poles: a child with too many names, yet sometimes feeling like none fully fit.

This has caused a kind of **identity crisis**. I often find myself grappling with whether I have entirely accepted who I am across these identities or whether I'm still seeking peace with the different parts of myself that my name represents.

The Spiritual Significance of Names

I once attended a workshop on name alignment led by Amy Jo Ellis of the Full Court of Atonement. She spoke of the importance of using the "right" name, especially when working with ancestral energies. This resonated deeply with me. Each name I carry seems to reflect a different aspect of myself—each one important, yet incomplete.

The **name alignment process** encouraged me to examine the energy of the names I use. **Gladys**, my childhood name, felt distant and uncomfortable, a name that didn't belong to me. **Lian**, meaning Lotus, on the other hand, resonates with my inner identity, the part of me that seeks growth, healing, and ascension.

But the real tension lies in the unresolved. I have not yet fully answered the question of **which name reflects my true self**. This journey through names feels like a search for self-acceptance, one that may never fully resolve but continues to shape my path.

Using **Dr. David Hawkins' Map of Consciousness**, I've begun to explore how names and identity influence our spiritual growth. To what extent do names hold us back, tethering us to past experiences and cultural expectations? How much freedom can I claim in choosing the name that reflects the person I am becoming?

As I continue this journey, I realize that names carry not just cultural or familial significance, but also the **power to shape our inner reality**. And while I still introduce myself as **Lian Henriksen**, the deeper search for alignment between my names and my identity continues—a quest for peace with the past and clarity about who I am in the present.

CHAPTER 21

My Inner Child & The Power and Beauty of Self-Acceptance

Written on 25th February 2024, 26th September 2024, and 2nd October 2024

Using **The Map of Consciousness** by **Dr. David Hawkins**, I discovered that my Chinese name **Geok Lian**, meaning **Jade Lotus**, vibrates at a frequency of **350 – Acceptance**, whereas **Gladys** aligns with a lower frequency of **250 – Neutrality**. My chosen name, **Lian**, meaning **Lotus**, vibrates at **390**, nearing the level of **Reason**.

What does Dr. Hawkins say about acceptance?

"At this level of awareness, a major transformation takes place, with the understanding that one is the source and creator of the experiences of one's life oneself."

The Inner Child and the Path to Self-Acceptance

My journey toward **self-acceptance** began long before I understood its true depth. It was only after my **cancer diagnosis** in **April 1999**, when I refused mainstream after-care, that I began exploring alternatives. Although I initially believed that my cancer was linked to a passionate love affair, it was the vivid dreams of my childhood during my recovery that pointed me toward deeper healing. These dreams reminded me of wounds that had been with me since childhood, wounds that I had yet to confront.

In the midst of my recovery, my sister, **Linda** sent me a brochure about the **Hoffman Quadrinity Process**, which emphasized the healing of the **Inner Child**. I instinctively knew that this was the course I needed. In **August 1999**, I attended the process in London, and it was here that I began the work of comforting my **Inner Child**—the part of me that carried so much unresolved pain.

At the end of the course, we were asked to confront our parents. In my case, it was my **mother**. I had long carried the memory of being frequently canned as a child. When I asked her why I had been treated this way, she replied, *"I don't really remember why, maybe because you were naughty or maybe because I was beaten myself."* Her response revealed a cycle of pain, passed down from one generation to the next.

It took many years for me to learn how to mother my **Inner Child**, to give her the love and compassion she had never received. The journey culminated on **New Year's Eve 2016/2017**, when I felt a sense of total forgiveness—not just for my mother, but for myself. It was as though the healing of my Inner Child was complete. This forgiveness was a profound moment of **self-acceptance**, where I understood that I could not change the past, but I could release its hold on me.

The Path to Self-Acceptance and Remorse

As I've continued working on **self-acceptance**, I've found that true **remorse** is a critical, yet often overlooked, part of this process. **Remorse** is not about guilt, shame, or self-pity; it is about feeling genuine sorrow for the past, without defensiveness or self-punishment. But why is feeling remorse so difficult?

Lazaris explains that the reason remorse is so hard to access is that most of us never had a foundation of remorse built into our emotional understanding. Or, if we did, it may have fallen into ruin over time. Without this foundation, we struggle to connect with our humanity in a way that allows for true forgiveness, growth, and healing.

Lazaris outlines **7 key points** that form the **foundation of being human**, a foundation necessary for feeling and embracing **remorse**:

1. **I can make mistakes. I am a human being. I can make mistakes.**
2. **I can forgive and I am forgivable.**
3. **Sometimes I am prepared and sometimes I am not, and this will be the way throughout my life. And it is okay.**
4. **My needs and wants, my preferences and my desires have value.**
5. **I can motivate myself out of my desire to grow. I know I have the basis and substance to build character, establish ideals, and uphold principles.**
6. **I can reach for my spirituality.**
7. **I have a piece of God/Goddess/All There Is within me. I am not separated from my spirituality.**

Building this foundation within myself has been crucial in my journey toward **self-acceptance** and in understanding that **remorse** is not something to fear but to embrace. It is part of what makes us human, allowing us to grow, forgive ourselves, and connect with our higher selves.

In many ways, working with my **Inner Child** has been a journey of **remorse** and **self-acceptance**. As I confronted my childhood experiences, I had to face the painful truth of the ways I had been hurt, and in doing so, I also had to forgive myself for the ways I had held onto that pain.

The Ongoing Process of Self-Acceptance

Since **2016**, I have been holding workshops, helping women build a foundation of **self-knowledge** and **spirituality**. Through this work, I have learned that **self-acceptance** is not something we achieve once and for all. It is a continuous process of learning, forgiving, and embracing both our imperfections and our potential. Working with remorse, and building this foundation, has allowed me to step more fully into my humanity and to live with greater compassion toward myself and others.

It has also allowed me to continue mothering my **Inner Child**—not as a task to be completed, but as an ongoing relationship that requires nurturing and care. **Self-acceptance** is about more than just forgiving the past; it is about learning to embrace all parts of ourselves, including the parts that were once broken or wounded.

The Spiritual Path Forward

Despite the progress I've made, this work is ongoing. Even after years of focusing on **self-mastery** and **self-love**, I still encounter moments where I must revisit old wounds and remind myself of these foundational truths. But now, with the understanding of **remorse** and **self-acceptance**, I can face these moments with more grace.

How do you approach the mistakes and regrets in your life? Do you have a foundation that allows you to forgive yourself, to feel remorse without shame, and to grow into a more accepting version of yourself?

As I continue my journey, I am committed to working with these principles, using them as a guide to live a life of **Purpose, Prosperity, Partnership, and Peace**—and to continue nurturing the **Inner Child** within me, as part of my lifelong commitment to **self-acceptance**.

CHAPTER 22

The Emotional Reflections on The Family Gathering Summer of July 2024

Written: 27th July 2024

On the 5th day, Sunday, July 21, 2024, the last day of Jo's and Jade's summer visit, only my daughters Jo and Karen, their children Josephine, Jade, and Anton, and I spent time together. During this time, I touched on an emotion that bothered me and made me very uncomfortable, but I couldn't describe it. Our lunch at McDonald's by the airport is best described as restrained. After I dropped Jo and Jade off, I went home and immediately posted in the WhatsApp Thread: "I wonder if we were able to create this sense of belonging to a family? And I wonder how important this feeling is, especially for the grandchildren?"

Only Jo replied: "I don't think we'll know until later, but at least we should try. 💜 So happy to have spent a little time with our Danish family!"

Despite some hiccups, the Denmark trip in the summer of 2024 was a success in many ways. However, one specific event during the gathering weighed heavily on me. Paolo, my son-in-law, didn't come at the last minute due to his mother's sudden illness. I was surprised when Jo decided to come alone with Jade. Throughout the gathering, she kept updating Paolo with many photos and messages, which meant he was still somewhat present, sending instructions on what Jade was NOT allowed to do. One particularly tense moment arose when Jade wasn't allowed to go horse riding with her Aunty Karen, who had looked forward to sharing that experience with her niece. This remote controlling irritated my son Kim, and I sensed that Jo felt judged.

This gathering brought up emotions for everyone, but it also made me wonder: *What unspoken expectations do we carry in our families, and how do those expectations impact our relationships?*

As I reflect on this, I can see how family dynamics—whether it's Jo trying to balance her relationship with Paolo while navigating her time with us, or the frustration of my other children—shape our experiences of belonging and acceptance. Family gatherings are not just about physical presence but also about navigating the emotional landscapes of everyone involved.

From my perspective, creating the family tree, an idea from Victoria, was the emotional climax of the gathering. It was a visual representation of my life: two marriages, one to a Chinese man and another to a Dane. Four children, two from each marriage, and six grandchildren. On July 23, I hung the tree in my bedroom and contemplated it. It stirred many uncomfortable emotions. At first, I thought it was regret—regret that I had married Boston, regret that my marriage to Bjørn hadn't fulfilled my dream of a perfect nuclear family. But the emotion was deeper and harder to name.

As I delved into my old notes, I was reminded of the importance of self-acceptance. My notes read: "Your resistance to receiving love is in direct proportion to your lack of self-acceptance." I realized that the uncomfortable emotions I was feeling were connected to my struggle with accepting myself, especially as I look back at the choices I've made and the impact they've had on my family.

Have you ever felt a deep, uncomfortable emotion that was hard to name? What might it be telling you about your relationship with yourself and others?

The Missing Piece: Remorse

Through reflection, I understood that the feeling I couldn't name was remorse, not regret. Remorse isn't about punishing oneself or feeling guilty—it's about feeling genuine sorrow for the pain I caused others, without being defensive or blaming. I've learned that without allowing myself to feel this deep sorrow, I cannot fully forgive myself or others, and without forgiveness, self-acceptance remains out of reach.

When was the last time you allowed yourself to feel true remorse, without falling into guilt or shame? How did it change your perspective on yourself or your relationships?

In this work, I've often found myself returning to old patterns of self-punishment instead of embracing compassion for myself. Despite my progress over the years, this family gathering reminded me that self-acceptance is an ongoing process, one that requires revisiting old wounds and approaching them with patience and forgiveness.

Seeking someone to listen, I reached out to Connie, a dear friend, to mirror my emotions. We discussed not only the pain of separation and family dynamics but also the roles we play—mother, daughter, grandmother, and spiritual guide. Connie, being an expert in Access Consciousness, encouraged me to ask open-ended questions, like: "What would it take to reconcile with the past?" and "What would it take to explore infinite choices with joy and ease?"

The Role of a Spiritual Teacher

Despite my children's skepticism about energy work, Connie reassured me that I have the tools to help heal the emotional wounds in my family, even if they don't share my beliefs. This gave me a sense of validation and reminded me that self-acceptance is not just about accepting my imperfections but also about trusting that I can help others, even when they may not fully understand or embrace my methods.

The Summer Gathering of 2024 highlighted the complexity of family dynamics—our unspoken judgments, our efforts to create belonging, and the discomfort that comes with unmet expectations. It also reaffirmed my commitment to self-acceptance, forgiveness, and letting go of rigid ideas about what family or life should look like. Life unfolds as it will, and my role is to continue working on The Art of Living Well.

In your own family, how do unspoken expectations affect your relationships? What steps might you take toward forgiveness, for yourself and others?

As I move forward, my prayer to the Divine Creator remains: Help me to be a Master in The Art of Living Well. Guide me to live a life filled with Purpose, Prosperity, Partnership, and Peace, and remind me that the journey is ongoing, filled with moments of discomfort but ultimately leading toward wholeness.

CHAPTER 23

My Soul Contracts with My Two Daughters

Written on: 27th Sept. 2024

The Summer Gathering with three of my four children in July stirred emotions that were both unsettling and hard to describe. On the final day of the gathering, my two daughters chose to spend time together without their brother, Kim. I found myself deeply uncomfortable because I could feel the pain my daughter had in her. This discomfort prompted me to look more closely at the **soul contracts** I share with each of my daughters, Jo and Karen, and to seek guidance from Nadia, a clairvoyant who helped me explore these spiritual agreements.

Soul contracts, as I have come to understand, are agreements made in the spiritual realm before we incarnate into this world. They guide our relationships and our life experiences, often bringing us face-to-face with the lessons we need to learn for our spiritual growth.

The Contract with Jo: My First Daughter

Nadia revealed that the **soul contract with Jo** is pivotal in my life. Jo has contracted to help me heal trauma and karma from my ancestral lineage. She is here to reveal my **shadow sides**, the parts of myself I don't want to confront. Through her, I am learning to see where I have hidden from my truth, to remove the masks I wear, and to embrace painful emotions—not just in myself but in others as well.

Our contract has deep roots. Nadia brought me back to a past life during the time of **Genghis Khan**, where I was a young boy forced to lead children into slavery, building bad karma by taking away their free will. In this lifetime, Jo's pain helps me confront that karma, forcing me to feel the loss and grief that others experienced when their children were taken away. **Her suffering is a mirror**, reflecting the deep healing I need to do for our lineage.

The Contract with Karen: My Second Daughter

Karen, my second daughter, has a different energy. Her soul contract is to help me **break down the walls of emotional hardness** that I built during my childhood. Karen carries a **soft, loving energy**—in contrast to Jo's sharp, powerful one—and her presence has always been a reminder of the love I need to nurture within myself. However, Karen has struggled with not feeling seen or heard during her childhood, particularly between the ages of 7 and 12.

Her role in my life is to **teach me self-love**, and to help me recognize my unconscious patterns of making myself invisible. It was hard for me to connect with her heart energy when she was born, and this has been a source of deep reflection for me. Yet, Karen's **softness is my salvation**; she is here to guide me toward embracing my vulnerability and to assist in completing my life's mission of **finding balance**—both within myself and in my relationships with others.

Transition to Family Dynamics

As I delved into the contracts with Jo and Karen, I realized that these **spiritual agreements** are not isolated to our private, internal worlds. They show up in the everyday dynamics of family life. The pain and challenges we face as a family—whether they come in the form of disagreements, unresolved tensions, or emotional outbursts—are reflections of the **deeper karmic contracts** we have with each other.

CHAPTER 24

Soul Contracts and Family Dynamics: Healing My Ancestral Lineage

Written on: 28th Sept. 2024

Understanding the soul contracts with my daughters opened my eyes to how **family dynamics** mirror the spiritual lessons I am meant to learn. The issues that arise within our family are **not mere accidents**; they are the playing out of deeper contracts and unresolved ancestral pain. When Karen expressed her concern about Victoria scolding Anton, or when Kim spoke of the trauma from our time in Portugal, I began to see how the **hiccups in our family relationships** are directly tied to the **soul agreements** we carry.

As I reflect on the soul contracts with my two daughters, described in **Chapter 23**, I begin to see how these spiritual agreements shape not only my inner world but also my external relationships. The lessons I am meant to learn from Jo and Karen have been unfolding in more subtle ways—through our daily interactions, through the small ruptures that arise in family dynamics. **The soul contracts are not confined to the metaphysical realm**; they ripple through the mundane, challenging me to live the lessons I've been tasked with mastering.

On **29th July 2024**, as I was working with DD on Jo's soul contract, she told me something that resonated deeply: "You are being called to heal your family lineage." This sentence lingers in my heart. **The weight of ancestral healing** has been with me for as long as I can remember, but DD's words brought it to the forefront. It's as though the conflicts, the pain, and even the love that I witness in my family are all part of this larger tapestry—threads woven together by past lives, karmic debts, and spiritual contracts that transcend time and space.

Karen's soul contract is to teach me self-love, to break down the walls of hardness that were built in my childhood. Her gentle heart energy contrasts sharply with Jo's piercing, powerful presence. And yet, both of them are guiding me toward the same goal: **to see myself clearly**, to stand strong within myself, and to heal the unspoken wounds passed down through generations.

On **21st September 2024**, when I invited Kim, Karen, and their families to complete the family tree, I didn't expect another hiccup in the family dynamics. Karen's comment that "Victoria scolds her son Anton all the time" stirred up emotions I hadn't anticipated. I could sense the **underlying tension**—something deeper than a mere disagreement. Was this part of the **soul contracts at play**, challenging us all to confront uncomfortable truths and unravel patterns that have been passed down?

The following conversation with Kim only confirmed my suspicions that **family pain runs deep**, and that it often takes the form of everyday disagreements. He expressed his concern about bringing up past trauma, specifically related to Portugal. He reminded me that "Portugal was a huge trauma for me and my family." His words struck a chord, not only because they were true but because they echoed the same karmic patterns I had been reflecting on with Jo's contract. We are all entangled in the web of **ancestral wounds**, and our relationships constantly bring these wounds to the surface.

Soul Contracts in Action: Navigating Family Hiccups

As I process these events, I realize that the **hiccups in family dynamics** are manifestations of the very contracts I've made with my children and perhaps even with Kim and the rest of my family. When Karen mentioned Victoria's treatment of Anton, it wasn't just an offhand remark—it was a mirror reflecting **our collective family pain**. Could it be that these conflicts are opportunities for deeper healing?

In the past, I might have seen these situations as isolated incidents, but now, with a clearer understanding of **soul contracts**, I see how they are all interconnected. **Jo's contract to help me clear my karma** and **Karen's contract to teach me self-love** both play out in these family dynamics. My response to the tension between Victoria and Anton, and Kim's feelings about past trauma, are not just responses to the present—they are part of a larger **ancestral healing** that is unfolding in real time.

Renegotiating the Soul Contract?

On **23rd September**, as DD suggested, I considered whether it was time to **renegotiate my soul contract**. Am I ready to continue bearing the weight of the family's karmic baggage? Or is it time to release some of this responsibility, to allow the younger generation—Karen, Jo, and even Kim—to take up their own roles in this spiritual journey? I feel the pull to **renegotiate**, not because I want to escape the work but because I recognize that healing is a collective effort. **We all have our contracts**, and mine is not to carry the entire lineage on my shoulders.

As I write this chapter, I realize that **every hiccup in family dynamics** is not a setback but an opportunity for growth. It's a reminder that the **soul contracts** we make with our loved ones are not just spiritual metaphors but living, breathing agreements that shape how we interact in the physical world. **Healing the ancestral lineage** is not a passive act—it's an ongoing process that requires all of us to confront our shadows, embrace our vulnerabilities, and ultimately, transform the pain into love.

A New Chapter: Integrating Spiritual Lessons with Family Dynamics

In this moment, I understand that **healing is not linear**. It doesn't happen all at once, nor does it unfold without conflict. The **soul contracts** I've made with Jo and Karen continue to teach me how to navigate these moments with grace, patience, and love. And, as I reflect on these recent hiccups in family dynamics, I see them as part of the same spiritual journey—a journey toward **wholeness and balance**, not just for myself but for the entire family.

CHAPTER 25

Inner Peace & Healing A War-Torn Legacy

Written on: 6th August 2024

A few days ago, I worked with FCOA Facilitator Deborah Danzeiser on speed calls for my daughter, Jo. When I showed Deborah my family tree, which I had made for my grandchildren, she commented that while the tree was beautiful, it didn't show my roots. It took me several days to gather photographs to represent the root level of my family. What struck me deeply during this process was that I had lost three of my grandparents to World War II. I was born on 8th July 1945, just one month before the atomic bombs were dropped on Hiroshima and Nagasaki, on the 6th and 9th of August, respectively. This realization felt like a profound moment—how deeply embedded is this legacy of war in my DNA? I cannot say for certain how it has shaped me, but I feel its presence in my life.

The next morning, during my silent hour, I was drawn to reflect on the 7th Keycode, White Buffalo Woman, from *The Sophia Code* by Kaia Ra. She speaks of the coming Age of Miracles and urges us all to become Sacred Living Peace Pipes, the *Chanunpa*. This teaching stirred something deep within me. How, I wondered, could I, in my own life, become a Sacred Living Peace Pipe, a channel for healing in a world still marked by the wounds of war? One path that came to mind was through Full Court of Atonement (FCOA) prayers.

A particular prayer surfaced in my memory:

"I, _____, place each and every world leader into a Full Court of Atonement for the purpose of resolving any and all reasons their

divine soul might be uncomfortable in their body and energy field. I ask for the amenable dissolution of this energy. I ask for divine intervention to assist in healing the hearts, spirits, and souls of each and every world leader."

But even with this prayer, I felt something was still missing. What will it truly take for global peace to become a reality for all people on Earth? The enormity of this question weighed on me, and I shared it in a Facebook post, accompanied by an image of peace.

Amy Jo Ellis responded to my post with a simple yet profound insight: *"Instead of looking for peace... we all have peace at moments."* She reminded me that peace is not something distant or elusive—it is present within each of us in small, fleeting moments. She also offered this prayer:

"I, _____, place each and every country, community, and tribe of the world into a Full Court of Atonement for the purpose of resolving any and all conflicts between us. I ask to create camaraderie, friendship, generosity, kindness, compassion, understanding, and acceptance among us all."

This resonated deeply with me. Perhaps the path to global peace lies in these small moments of inner peace, shared between individuals and communities. If more of us experience these moments of peace, they might ripple outward, eventually leading to a more peaceful world. But again, what do I know except to ask my soul and divinity for guidance?

Coincidentally, around this time, I became more active in the Global Grandmothers' Council Network on Facebook. At 79, I feel that I am entering a new phase of life—Spiritual Elderhood. This is a time to become a master of two worlds, which, to me, means mastering duality. On 22nd July 2024, I made this post in the group:

"As I watched the Family Tree being created, I couldn't help but reflect on my own feelings and emotions. I wonder if I will ever need to apologize to my grandchildren for the times I was hard to understand, accept, appreciate, love, or validate. I felt this need constantly with my own children."

The responses I received from fellow grandmothers were deeply moving. Each shared their own struggles and realizations, offering comfort and wisdom:

- **Lesa Williams** shared: *"Oh yes, I raised my 12 kids in a Christian cult—10 sons and two daughters. I had much to undo. I spent years taking responsibility and deeply apologizing for the pain I had caused. Now, I've drawn boundaries and let them know they can't constantly throw things at me anymore because my love for them is greater than my mistakes. Healing isn't linear, but our times together are much smoother now."*

- **Claudia Cane Garrett** said: *"Sadly, our children don't always appreciate who we are. Mothers are all on a sacred journey shaped by our life and times. Our history isn't always celebrated in our time on Earth."*

- **Nadine Erikson** added: *"I've made many mistakes, and I've taken responsibility for them. I think many of us would like a do-over, but we get another chance with our grandchildren."*

- **Caryn Devlin** reflected: *"Every generation has things that could have been done better. As humans evolve, we* *improve. By keeping our history intact, we can see how far we've come and the lessons we've learned. As they say, when you know better, you do better."*

- Finally, **Sarah Emoteth** shared: *"I've done a decade of repentance work. Now, my way to bless my grandchildren is by not judging their parents for what I taught them. I hold faith that we will one day know ourselves, forgive, and repent for the damages done. I want to be a safe place for my grandchildren that I didn't know how to be for my children."*

I thanked Sarah for her wisdom and asked if she succeeded in being that safe space for her grandchildren. She replied:

"I did talk therapy for 25 years. My husband left after 25 years of marriage, and I fell into a deep depression. Only one therapist created a safe space for me to go back to my inner child and express what had been stuck for so long. That moment was life-changing. Now, I do my own inner child work so I can be that safe place for my grandchildren. When a soul radiates fearlessness about feeling emotions, others sense it. That's why my grandsons love having me around—I am a safe space for them to express what they need to."

Her words affirmed the importance of creating a space for emotional healing, not just for myself but for my grandchildren as well.

On 3rd August, I made another post about my experience listening to my audiobook, *The Sophia Code* by Kaia Ra, specifically the 7th Keycode, White Buffalo Woman. In it, White Buffalo Woman speaks of the coming Age of Miracles and urges us all to become Sacred Living Peace Pipes, the *Chanunpa*. She also speaks of the Sky

Grandmothers, reminding us that prayers are our greatest medicine. This brought me back to my experience meditating on the red soil plateaus of Sedona, Arizona, about 10 years ago. I couldn't help but wonder if I had connected with her spirit then, though I can't be sure.

I asked in my post if any other grandmothers had a connection with White Buffalo Woman and would be willing to share their prayers.

Mayana Kingery responded: *"A message from White Buffalo Woman came through to me during a ceremony on 12/12/2010. She said, 'Honor the traditions of the Natives, but don't get stuck in them. Go beyond the traditions into your nativity.'"*

Her words sparked something in me. *Our nativity is the stars.* One day, I will understand what this means in my own life. Reading Ken Carey's *Return of the Bird Tribes* and Marlo Morgan's *Mutant Message Down Under* further deepened my understanding of this cosmic connection.

On 7th August 2024, Amy Jo Ellis reminded me of a post she had made in 2021 about resolving world conflicts through the "5-R's"—Rage, Resentment, the need for Retaliation, the need for Revenge, and the need for Restitution. She proposed that we work as a community to use the Full Court of Atonement to resolve these issues on a global scale.

Amy Jo wrote:

"I, _____, place each and every leader of each and every country on Earth into a Full Court of Atonement for the purpose of Soul Recognition and Absorbed Sibling Resolution. I ask to resolve any and all reasons for the need for revenge, retaliation, restitution, rage, resentment, greed, jealousy, supremacy, murder, and war. I

ask to analyze their timelines and resolve any and all reasons for war. I ask to resolve any and all reasons preventing them from experiencing altruism, kindness, philanthropy, compassion, generosity, understanding, and acceptance of others."

In her post, Amy Jo also included the advisors to these leaders, asking for the same resolution. I felt that this was particularly timely, as it was the 79th anniversary of the Hiroshima and Nagasaki bombings. I added myself to the FCOA prayer, realizing that including myself made the prayer feel more complete, more human—less self-righteous.

This process reminds me of a profound moment during my visit to the Wailing Wall in Jerusalem on New Year's Day, 2018. I had asked, "What is the solution to wars?" The answer that came back to me was simple yet deeply revealing:

Be aware of your inner passive aggression.

It was an answer that forced me to look inward and confront the shadows I carry—the self-righteousness, the need to be right, the subtle ways in which I hold on to conflict, even as I strive for peace. I am learning that true peace, both within myself and in the world, requires more than just prayers and good intentions. It demands that I take responsibility for the energies I carry, for the way I contribute to the collective consciousness.

Yet, as I reflect on this journey, I realize that my personal healing is not just for me. It extends beyond the bounds of my own life and reaches into the lives of those I love—my children, my grandchildren, and the generations to come. Each moment of peace I cultivate, each shadow I confront, is a seed planted in the soil of future legacies. I have inherited a legacy of war and loss, but I now see that I have the power to transform that legacy into one of peace and healing.

This work is slow, often invisible, like the growth of mycelium underground. But just as mycelium connects the roots of trees and supports the entire ecosystem, so too does this healing spread, quietly and persistently, through the connections we make. It starts with inner peace—mine, yours, each of ours—and from there, it grows.

As I move forward, I understand that the journey is not mine alone. I am part of a greater web of healing, a mycelium network that spans the world. Through this work, I join with others, like the grandmothers in the Global Grandmothers' Council Network, to nurture the spirit of future generations. The seeds we plant today will grow into the forest of tomorrow.

And so, with this awareness, I step into the next phase of this journey—seeding the mycelium, one connection at a time.

CHAPTER 26

My Grandchildren & Seeding the Mycelium

9th August 2024

Yesterday marked the **Lion's Gate Portal 8/8/8**, a powerful day for spiritual alignment. In addition to nurturing the spirit of my youngest grandchild, **Wilbur**, I participated in the **Global Grandmothers Council Network's event, 8/8/8 Mycelium Seeding**.

The term **mycelium** refers to the intricate underground network of fungal threads that spread beneath the earth, connecting plants and enabling the exchange of nutrients and information. In many ways, **mycelium serves as a spiritual metaphor**—it represents the **hidden, yet powerful connections** that form between people, generations, and communities. Just as mycelium nourishes and supports ecosystems, we too form a web of **spiritual nourishment and wisdom**, particularly through our roles as grandmothers.

By seeding the mycelium, we are planting **spiritual wisdom, love, and protection** that will spread through future generations, connecting and nurturing them in ways that may not always be visible but are deeply impactful.

At this event, I met a young grandmother from Poland. Our connection felt like the beginning of something important. Whether we collaborate under the **Danish branch of the Global Grandmothers Council** or independently, I know we are destined to help ourselves and other grandmothers *"age gracefully."*

Being part of this **Global Grandmothers' Council Network** has been invaluable. It has connected me with women who share a common purpose: **to be protectors of the spirit of their grandchildren**. But what does it truly mean to **protect the spirit** of our grandchildren?

Protecting the Spirit of Our Grandchildren

To be a protector of the spirit of our grandchildren means **guarding their sacred essence**—their natural curiosity, joy, and fearlessness—from the unconscious patterns and **emotional wounds** that we may unintentionally pass down. As elders and caregivers, we must recognize the ways in which our unresolved **feelings of inferiority, guilt, shame**, and **repressed memories** can be projected onto them, shaping their sense of self and the world around them.

Many of us carry the **emotional baggage** of past generations—unhealed traumas, limiting beliefs, and the weight of cultural or societal expectations. Without awareness, these unresolved emotions can be projected onto our grandchildren, influencing how we guide and nurture them. For example:

- A grandparent who carries **feelings of inadequacy** may unintentionally communicate these insecurities to their grandchildren, affecting how they see themselves and their potential.
- **Unresolved fears** from our own lives may cause us to overprotect or interfere in ways that limit their freedom to explore and discover their own path.

To truly protect their spirit, we must:

1. **Break the Cycle of Projection**: By becoming aware of and healing our own wounds, we ensure that our grandchildren are not burdened by the same **emotional patterns**.

Protecting their spirit means creating a space where they are free to grow without the weight of our unresolved pain.

2. **Allow Their Spirit to Flourish**: It's not about controlling their path but about nurturing their **natural fearlessness** and freedom to become who they are meant to be. We protect their spirit by ensuring they can explore the world with openness and confidence.

3. **Empower Them Through Love and Acceptance**: When we engage with them from a place of **unconditional love**, rather than fear or control, we give them the **emotional space** to fully express themselves and develop into their true potential.

4. **Heal Ourselves to Heal Them**: By doing our own inner work, we liberate them from carrying the burdens of previous generations. We become the link that breaks the chain of generational pain, allowing them to step into a future of wholeness.

This is why being part of the **Global Grandmothers Council** has been so valuable to me. It is a community of women who are dedicated to this sacred work—**protecting the spirit** of their grandchildren and ensuring that future generations are free from the emotional chains of the past.

In this context, I want to share the wisdom of **Grandmother Three Crows**, who spoke about the purity and fearlessness of newborn children:

"All children are born fearless. A newborn child is open, in awe of everything—without fear, self-doubt, or prejudice. He is just being, *experiencing, looking, feeling. Every moment is an adventure, free and fearless, without judgment. This sacred little being loves unconditionally, without judgment of others.*

He has his own instincts—natural, pure, and sacred. **We all start this way**, *but depending on where we land in life, the journey begins toward being trained out of that purity. Slowly, we are taught self-loathing, self-harm, and self-doubt. We are led to believe we are insignificant, unlovable, or unimportant, and some of us carry these beliefs for our entire lives.*

This, in turn, prevents us from becoming who we are meant to be, from living fully in our sacredness, preciousness, and uniqueness."

Grandmother Three Crows reminds us that this is the **spiritual battle** all human beings face, living in the **third and fourth dimensions of duality. Earth is a school**—a place where we learn about suffering and the purpose it serves. The challenge for us is to awaken to the truth of **oneness with all that is**.

The Path to the Fifth Dimension

How do we rise out of this **chaos and suffering** into the **fifth dimension**, where unity and peace reign? The answer is not simple, and it certainly doesn't come with the wave of a wand. It requires **discipline, courage, and hard work**. We must embrace our shadows and actively participate in life's lessons.

From my own experience, I've learned that the key is not to take sides. There is something much bigger unfolding, something beyond the surface-level conflicts of duality. We are, as **Grandmother Three Crows** and others have said, here to learn about chaos and duality in this **Earth school**.

Embracing the Shadows

As **Yongey Mingyur Rinpoche** teaches:

"Wherever we are, whatever we do, all we need to do is recognize our thoughts, feelings, and perceptions as something natural. Neither rejecting nor accepting, we simply acknowledge the experience and let it pass. If we keep this up, we'll eventually find ourselves able to manage situations we once found painful, scary, or sad. We'll discover a sense of confidence that isn't rooted in arrogance or pride. We'll realize that we're always sheltered, always safe, always home."

These words resonate deeply with me. By acknowledging our experiences without judgment, we move closer to the freedom we seek.

The Key to Saving the World

Ultimately, the question remains: **What is the key to saving the world?**

The answer lies within you.

You are the key.

Heal yourself.
Know yourself.
Make yourself whole and free.
Release all limits so that your love can flow unconditionally—for yourself and for the world.
This will open the heaven of your heart completely, and it will guide you without fail.
—Yung Pueblo

This is what I believe, too. The journey of healing starts within, and through that personal transformation, we unlock the potential to heal the world.

CHAPTER 27

The Finished Family Tree & If I Must Die

Written on 22nd Sept. 2024

Sitting at the art and sound installation titled *"Sound of Becoming: Another Kind of Being – Living-Dying"* on 20th September 2024, I was drawn to a poem that felt like it had been waiting for me. *"If I Must Die"* by Refaat Alareer, a poet who, along with his family, perished in an Israeli airstrike in 2023, resonated deeply with me. Born the same year as my son Kim, Alareer's words echoed a truth I have grappled with as I approach my 80th birthday.

If I must die,
Let it bring hope,
Let it be a tale.

Sitting this morning, gazing at the completed family tree, I was filled with gratitude for the life I've lived and the legacy I am leaving behind. Alareer's poem crystallized what I felt in my bones. As I stand on the precipice of the next phase of my journey, I recognize that my story—my life—is more than just a collection of moments. It is a tale. And if I must die, let that tale bring hope. Let it be a bridge.

The Tale of My Life: Forgiveness and Healing

Over the years, my life's purpose has become clearer. The **soul contracts** I've explored with my sons and daughters, the healing of ancestral lineage, and my reflections have all led me to this point. My life has not been without its pain, conflicts, or family hiccups, but in the end, it has been about **growth—mine, my children's, and the healing of my ancestors**.

Part of this healing process has extended beyond my family. In 2003, while living in **Hanoi**, I had the chance to work with children who were third-generation victims of **Agent Orange**, the toxic chemical used during the Vietnam War. These children carried the scars of a conflict that occurred long before they were born. I visited them regularly at the **Children's Hospital**, teaching them art. Their drawings were a poignant expression of innocence and resilience, and they moved me deeply.

Wanting to do something more, I turned their artwork into **Christmas cards**, which we sold to raise funds. The proceeds allowed us to take the children to a **water puppet show**—a joyful day that remains vivid in my memory. Watching their faces light up, I was reminded that even amidst the worst tragedies, there is always space for **joy and healing**.

But what struck me most about my time in **Vietnam wasn't** just the children's resilience—the forgiveness radiated from the Vietnamese people. Despite the horrors of war and the lasting effects of Agent Orange, they had chosen to forgive. They moved forward, not clinging to hatred but embracing life with a spirit of **reconciliation** that I struggled to comprehend then.

This experience planted a seed in me that has grown over the years and taken root as I reflect on my life's journey. I've come to realize that **healing**—whether within families or between nations—requires a willingness to **forgive**, even when the pain seems too deep to bear. This lesson resonates with me today as I look at global conflicts like the war between **Ukraine and Russia**, and my heart aches when I see the Danish government's involvement in supporting war. I wonder, where is the space for **forgiveness**? Where is the room for **reconciliation**?

A Bridge Between Worlds

This thread of **healing and forgiveness** has woven itself through much of my life. I've witnessed division firsthand, from the **racial riots in Malaysia** in 1967 to the ongoing conflict in **Palestine and Israel**. These experiences have shown me how differences—whether racial, religious, or cultural—can tear communities apart. Yet, they have also revealed the profound power of reconciliation, bridging divides and bringing people together.

Reflecting on my life, I recognize that the **healing of my family lineage** is just one piece of the puzzle. There is a more significant calling—a need to **heal societal wounds**, just as I have worked to heal the personal ones. My vision for **Talking and Listening Circles** between **Muslim and non-Muslim grandmothers** and their grandchildren stems from this more profound realization. Just as stories helped me understand the children's humanity in Vietnam, I believe sharing our stories can help us see each other with compassion across race, culture, and religion divides.

A Final Chapter of Hope

As I sit here, looking at the completed **family tree**, I realize that my story—like the family tree itself—is a tale of **healing and hope**. My experiences, whether in Vietnam or within my own family, have shown me that **forgiveness** is the foundation of peace. If I must die, let it not be with unfinished work. Let the seeds I have planted in my family and the hearts of others continue to grow into something greater than myself.

This final chapter is not an ending but a beginning—for my family, future generations, and the communities I hope to touch. Just as **Refaat Alareer's words** will live on in the hearts of those who hear them, so too will my story live on through those I leave behind.

If I must die,
Let it bring hope.
Let it be a tale.

CHAPTER 28

The Midwives of Peace

Midwives of Peace is a community I created six months ago to offer **Healing through Listening and Storytelling Circles**. Our mission is to foster a community of **trust, hope, faith, and inner peace** within ourselves and among members. The peace we create in ourselves is our gift to the world—a contribution toward a new world waiting to be born.

The Midwives of Peace Experience: This community is a safe space for women who recognize themselves as souls having a human experience and wish to deepen their spiritual exploration. Here, we connect our inner spiritual lives with our outer lives of action. We share our stories, strengths, and vulnerabilities, knowing we are seen with compassionate eyes. Together, we cultivate deeper connections with our souls, honoring our needs, setting boundaries, and healing past wounds.

Our Tool: *Listening*. Through my own experiences, I have learned that compassionate listening brings clarity and healing. When we listen with our hearts, the wounds hidden within us begin to heal, bringing us peace.

Recently, a powerful experience deepened my sense of purpose with **Midwives of Peace**. On **29th September 2024**, I attended a **Global Grandmothers' Council Network** fundraising event where **Grandmother Gayle Crosmaz**, a shaman trained by the **Inuits of Greenland**, shared her story. She then began to drum, an ancient practice meant to awaken the **Dragon Energy** within us. As the drumbeat filled the room, I felt a stirring in my spirit that I hadn't experienced in years.

This wasn't my first connection to Greenland. Throughout my 42 years life in Denmark, people have asked me if I was a **Greenlander** or **Eskimo**—a question that surfaced again just the day before at a recent art installation. I have always felt irritated which for me meant, an inexplicable connection, but it was that evening, with the drumbeats resonating through me, that I understood it on a deeper level.

The next morning, I woke with a clear calling to revive the work I had started 10 years ago, with **Initiatives of Change, a Swiss based organisation**—a mission to heal the strained relationship between the **African Muslims** and the **White Danes of Denmark**. This calling, awakened by **Grandmother Gayle's** drumming, feels like an extension of the work I do with **Midwives of Peace**. It is about fostering **reconciliation, compassion, and unity**—not only within ourselves but within our communities and the world.

In **Midwives of Peace**, we work together to cultivate healing by listening deeply to one another's stories. Inspired by these experiences, I am reminded that **true peace begins within** but expands outward, touching the lives around us. My hope is that each member of this community, through her own healing journey, can contribute to a collective peace, building a world where unity is woven from our differences, and healing comes from the compassion we offer each other.

Afterword

The Golden Keys to My Heaven on Earth

I accept that I hold the Golden Keys to my Heaven on Earth.

I accept that I create my reality by the Power of my Own Word.

My Word is Good, My Heart is Pure.

By the Loving Power of My Pure Words, I now create my Heaven on Earth.

At 79, as I reflect on my life, I see a journey of continuous transformation. From my cancer recovery in 1999 to becoming The Silver Crone from Denmark, every step has been about self-discovery, healing, and reclaiming my inner power. Each chapter has led me to this moment of freedom, compassion, and a deep, abiding peace.

Yet, my journey toward peace is still unfolding. On 1st September 2024, while contemplating Gene Key #40, I was reminded that the path from Exhaustion to the Siddhi of Divine Will comes through Resolve. Though I accept that I hold the Golden Keys to my Heaven on Earth, I now face a new realization: that everything in life—whether it happens to us or around us—unfolds according to the Divine Will of God.

This truth is delicate, yet profound. To accept that all events are an expression of Divine Will is to embrace a peace that goes beyond understanding. Divine Will invites us to relax so deeply into our human experience that we begin to shine with light. It's a reminder that one day, each of us will surrender our ego to the whole, and in that surrender, we find true liberation.

This realization feels like the next step in a journey I've been on for many years. In May 2021, I received a message from the Akashic Records that brought clarity to the purpose of this book:

"This book is about Freedom.

Freedom to be who you truly are.

Freedom to express yourself in the world.

Freedom to stand up for injustice.

This book is about Compassion...

It's a story of moving from victimhood to freedom."

These words have been my guide. They remind me that my story isn't just mine. It's for anyone who resonates with the journey from pain to peace, from constraint to liberation. My struggles, my lessons, my victories—they belong to all who seek freedom.

Now, as I look ahead, I feel ready for whatever comes next—whether in this life or beyond. I trust in my divinity and the path that has brought me here. My life is filled with love and light, and I am at peace.

To you, dear reader, I invite you to look within. What parts of your journey are calling for healing? What aspects of yourself are waiting for freedom? May you, too, find your own Heaven on Earth, shaped by the unique beauty of your path.

Acknowledgments

Writing this book has been a deeply transformative experience, and I am immensely grateful to those who have supported and guided me along the way.

To **my daughters, Jo and Karen**, you have each been my greatest teachers, showing me the depths of love, healing, and self-awareness. Your journeys have inspired much of my own, and for that, I am deeply thankful.

To **my younger sister Linda**, whose unwavering pursuit of becoming the best version of herself, despite her material success, continues to inspire me. Your humility and dedication to growth are something I admire greatly.

To **my sons, Kim and Kenneth**, who have walked their paths with courage and strength. You have been my grounding force and the source of so many of my life's lessons. Thank you for your love, patience, and unwavering support.

I am deeply grateful to **the Council of Light** and the guidance I have received through the **Akashic Records**, which gave me clarity and purpose throughout this journey. Your wisdom has illuminated my path, helping me find the courage to share my story.

To **Connie Kelly**, my mirror and reflection partner, thank you for being there as a constant source of truth, helping me to see myself more clearly. Your presence has been invaluable to my journey of self-discovery.

To the many **women I have mentored**, especially those navigating single motherhood, thank you for trusting me with your stories.

Your strength and resilience have inspired me, and you have shown me the true power of transformation.

I would also like to express my deep appreciation to **Amy Jo Ellis** and **Karen McMullen**, whose teachings and wisdom have had a profound influence on my journey. Your insights have greatly shaped my understanding of the human spirit and our potential for growth.

Finally, to **my readers**, who have taken the time to read this book, I hope it brings you peace, insight, and a deeper connection to your own journey. May it serve as a reminder that healing is possible, and that we all hold the power to transform our lives.

With deep love and gratitude,

Lian Henriksen

Website: https://lianhenriksen.com/
e.mail: lian.henriksen2009@gmail.com
Facebook: https://www.facebook.com/lian.henriksen.7/
Instagram: https://www.instagram.com/lianhenriksen.silvercrone/
YouTube: https://www.youtube.com/@lianhenriksen4236